CONFRONTING THE STIGMA
IN THEIR LIVES

CONFRONTING THE STIGMA IN THEIR LIVES

Helping People With A Mental Retardation Label

By

JAMES R. DUDLEY, PH.D.

With a Foreword by

Robert B. Edgerton, Ph.D.

CHARLES C THOMAS • PUBLISHER, LTD.
Springfield • Illinois • U.S.A.

Published and Distributed Throughout the World by
CHARLES C THOMAS • PUBLISHER, LTD.
2600 South First Street
Springfield, Illinois 62794-9265

© *1997 by* CHARLES C THOMAS • PUBLISHER, LTD.
ISBN 0-398-06737-6 (cloth)
ISBN 0-398-06738-4 (paper)
Library of Congress Catalog Card Number: 96-37186

Printed in the United States of America
SC-R-3

Library of Congress Cataloging-in-Publication Data

Dudley, James R.
    Confronting the stigma in their lives : helping people with a
mental retardation label / by James R. Dudley ; with a foreword by
Robert B. Edgerton.
        p.   cm.
    Includes bibliographical references and index.
    ISBN 0-398-06737-6 (cloth). — ISBN 0-398-06738-4 (pbk.)
    1. Mentally handicapped—Psychology. 2. Mentally handicapped—
Social conditions. 3. Discrimination against the handicapped.
4. Stigma (Social psychology) I. Title.
HV3004.D85   1997
362.3'8—dc21   96-37186
                                                                              CIP

To My Mother and Father

*Who were the first people in my life
to teach me to value and love differences in others.*

FOREWORD

The acclaimed motion picture, *Forest Gump*, did much to valorize the life of a man born with an IQ that qualified him for the label of a person with mental retardation but nevertheless attended regular public school classes, then became a collegiate football star, decorated war hero, millionaire, and spiritual role model. The real world has all too seldom allowed persons with low intellectual abilities to live as fully as others, much less to achieve such wondrous things. There are some small-scale societies known to the ethnographic record that have favorably treated people with what we can gloss as mental retardation, but many others stigmatize and often brutalize these people. So it has been in Europe, China, and the Americas, including the United States. In recent years, the brutality has lessened, but stigma continues to play a central and painful role in the lives of people who are labeled mentally retarded.

To this day, "mental retardation" (not to mention its many colloquial synonyms) is as wounding a label as anyone can experience. Even the well-intentioned and often effective "disabilities movement" has not yet reached out to embrace persons with that label as integral members of their counsels, as many persons once labeled "mentally retarded" with whom I have worked for almost 40 years have pointed out with some bitterness. My first experience with persons labeled with mental retardation involved a naturalistic study of young adults who had earlier been released from a large state hospital for what were then known diagnostically as "mental defectives." As these people did their best to adapt to life in nearby communities without help from the officials who had incarcerated them yet taught them no social living skills, they experienced many difficulties, but none so painful or pervasive as their ever-present realization that they were thought by society to be mental "defectives" who were so incompetent that they had been hospitalized as persons unable to care for themselves. Their early post-hospital lives were spent attempting to deny to themselves that they were "mentally retarded" and to pass as normal in the eyes of people who did not know their backgrounds. I cannot forget the words of one suffering young woman who told me that "I have a tendency of an ailment, but it's not what it seems." Later, I found that stigma, passing, and denial tormented the lives of many other persons labeled with mental retardation, including persons from ethnic minority backgrounds whose tears I am unlikely to forget.

No one understands the life experiences of persons labeled with mental retardation better than Dr. James R. Dudley. His 1983 book, *Living with Stigma,* is a powerfully evocative portrayal of the worlds in which these stigmatized people live. This current book returns to the lives of persons with a mental retardation label telling us again how they cope with stigmatization. But it is far more than another look at stigmatized lives. It carefully examines the ways in which stigma is promoted and how stigma should be confronted if it is someday to be eliminated. Based on more than 15 years of research and personal involvement, Dr. Dudley proposes specific ways that labeled persons can act to reduce the stigma in their lives. He also looks insightfully at self-advocacy groups and the mental retardation system itself, one that too often unwittingly promotes stigma. He offers a detailed prescription for a stigma-free mental retardation service system and for helping labeled persons make the transition away from that system. Dr. Dudley understands how much words can wound and he suggests many helpful approaches to the reduction of stigma based on labels. He also knows that there must be deeds as well, and his proposals for changing the world in which we all live with the stigma of mental retardation labels are as practical as they are humane. No one with an interest in mental retardation or disability in general should miss this book.

ROBERT B. EDGERTON, PH.D.
University of California, Los Angeles

PREFACE

This book is for "allies" of people with a mental retardation label who want to confront and eliminate the problem of stigma. Allies are practitioners and administrators, board members, students, family members, and people with disabilities. Some allies are trained in professional disciplines like social work, psychology, special education, and nursing; and others are volunteers. Some work in the developmental disabilities field and others do not. Most important, allies care about people with disabilities and genuinely want to help them overcome stigma.

The book is a sequel to an earlier book, *Living with Stigma: The Plight of the People Who We Label Mentally Retarded*, published in 1983. Based on a participant-observation study, that book described the stigma problems debilitating the lives of 27 adults with mental retardation labels and how they coped with these problems. This book makes frequent reference to the study reported in that book, including many quotes from the research subjects. In most cases, the quotes from labeled people in *Living with Stigma* are not referenced.

In this book, I revisit the problem of stigma. I examine this social problem several years later and share much of my work that has focused on confronting stigma. I also draw on the innovative work of many others. In addition, a very special feature throughout the book is the inclusion of the voices of people labeled with mental retardation. Indeed, their stories and viewpoints reflect a central message of the book—that they must be heard and taken more seriously!

This book explores how we can help *all* people with a mental retardation label. This problem is debilitating and oppressive regardless of the level of one's functioning. Yet, many sections of the book primarily reflect the experiences of people who have mild or moderate retardation labels. They voice their concerns more freely than people with severe disabilities, and more is known about how they manage their stigma encounters. Also, most projects designed to combat stigma have focused on them because it is presumed that they have the greatest potential for achieving societal inclusion. However, while much less is known about the stigma problems of people with more severe disabilities, the reader is encouraged to use the book to confront their stigma problems as well. The perspective and approach of the book are intended for this important work.

The overall aim of the book is to understand, confront, and overcome the problem of stigma. The book is divided into two parts. In Part I, the book provides understanding about this insidious social problem and its harmful effects on people with disabilities. Part II is devoted to several ways of confronting and overcoming stigma.

I begin the book with a brief first chapter that inquires how we should refer to people with a mental retardation label. I emphasize the power of language and labels in identifying people, and I explain why I have decided to give special attention to this issue in the book.

In Chapter 2, I explore the significance of stigma as we approach the end of the twentieth century. The chapter inquires why so little has been written about stigma while much more attention has been given to related topics like normalization, valued roles, and quality of life. A socio-anthropological perspective is offered to prepare the reader for later chapters.

Because I believe that stigma is a problem that virtually everyone can be guilty of perpetrating, I close Chapter 2 with personal questions for the reader to ponder. I invite the reader to continue to examine his or her personal issues at other stages of the book because I believe that confronting stigma involves doing personal work as well as changing other people and institutions.

We cannot succeed in confronting the stigma associated with intellectual disabilities without having an intimate understanding of what it is. The next four chapters focus on the nature of stigma and its effects on people with disabilities. These chapters define and describe stigma largely from the perspective of people with a mental retardation label. Numerous illustrations are included to illuminate what stigma means to them.

In *Living with Stigma*, I identified several important themes that illuminate stigma's existence. Many of these themes have also been reported in other research studies. Such studies have typically used qualitative research methods and involved the long-term involvement of a researcher in the lives of the subjects. In addition, I have become aware that many self-advocates have articulated some of these themes at their conferences and in their articles and newsletters. These pertinent themes are highlighted in Chapters 3 to 6.

Chapter 3, "The Promotion of Stigma," describes a variety of ways that stigma is promoted by individuals, organizations, and institutions. These stigma-promoting acts have been identified by labeled people and others.

Chapter 4 is titled "A Separate World." This chapter describes a social world that has little interchange with the so-called "normal world." The friendships of people in this separate world are largely restricted to others with similar labels, and family members and staff members employed to help them. Their activities are typically segregated with regards to their housemates, work, leisure and recreation, and other everyday experiences. A "wall" of stigma precludes a more normalized life. There are, of course, exceptions where a wall is not evident, and some of these breakthroughs to the "normal world" are also described.

Chapter 5 highlights important feelings and attitudes of labeled people toward their disabilities, labels, and stigma. The studies that are cited reveal that adults with labels of mild and moderate retardation, in particular, have keen awareness of their disabilities and the challenges that their disabilities impose. They are also keenly aware of the stigma in their lives, including the stigma associated with labels.

Recognizing that many people with a mental retardation label have their own developed perceptions of their personal and social circumstances, Chapter 6 explores how they have learned to cope with stigma. Five different coping strategies are described and illustrated. The potential that people have for utilizing these strategies is also considered.

A major emphasis of this book is on offering ideas for confronting and overcoming this debilitating problem. Thus, Part II moves from understanding stigma to confronting it. Chapter 7 describes a general approach for confronting stigma. One central guideline of this approach is that stigma problems and disability-related problems must be distinguished and addressed differently. A second guideline is that labeled people must be central participants in any effort to confront stigma.

Chapters 8 to 12 describe specific approaches to confronting stigma. Chapter 8 focuses on promoting friendships between people with and without disabilities. A special project is described that offers opportunities for students or staff members to develop friendships with labeled people and exposure to their stigma problems. A major premise of this chapter is that promoting friendships must be central to any successful effort to confront stigma.

Chapter 9 focuses on the work that people with a mental retardation label must do with each other. This "private work" is conducted in peer groups where needs and concerns related to stigma are shared. Problem-solving, support, and consciousness-raising are emphasized in these groups and the taboos to discussing their disabilities, labels, and stigma problems are challenged. Questions are included for labeled people to consider as they discuss their private work. Specific group illustrations are also included.

The self-advocacy movement is highlighted in Chapter 10. This movement, which I identify as one of the most significant in recent United States history, is described and its achievements assessed. Suggestions are proposed for assisting self-advocates and recruiting new members to the movement.

Chapter 11 focuses on a major promoter of stigma, the mental retardation system. A plan for eliminating stigma from the mental retardation system is proposed. Numerous questions are identified for agencies to consider in assessing whether or not they are perpetrators of stigma. Several empowering roles are highlighted for consumers, including being helpers, advisors, and researchers.

A relatively large number of people with a mental retardation label are suspected of being no longer in need of the mental retardation system. Yet, this reality seems to be largely ignored, and these consumers continue to remain dependent and unprepared for the "outside" world. In Chapter 12, a delabeling process is described for helping them leave. The work of "passing" is a focus—helping some people with disabilities to pass as someone with a less stigmatic label. The drawbacks and risks of this work are discussed as well. A set of transitional services is recommended that prepares them to develop more normalized and valued lives.

In the Epilogue, I review the options available to people with a mental retardation label, and explore the book's implications for other socially oppressed groups, including people with physical disabilities and people with mental illness.

ACKNOWLEDGMENTS

First, I would like to acknowledge many people with disabilities for helping make this book possible. Some of them were the subjects of my research or participants of the projects that I conducted. Others were authors of their own articles and books, or research subjects of other studies that I have cited. Each of them has taught me in very personal ways about stigma, and they have always convinced me that I am investigating something very important to them. I wish that I could name each one of them to give them the credit that they richly deserve. Yet, most of them remain unnamed to protect their privacy.

Countless other people have helped me in the preparation of the book. Over the past 15 years, I have worked with several people on pertinent projects. While I cannot identify all of them, I particularly remember and thank Heather McLennan, Steve Dorsey, Susan Willamson, Jasmin Vasquez, Susanne DiSanto, and Irv Segal. I also thank Temple University and faculty of the School of Social Administration for encouraging me to offer some of these projects to my students.

Several people helped with the review of various sections of the book. Karen Stevens freely gave time from her busy schedule to review several ideas in the book with her staff at the Integration Network of Western Massachusetts; she also provided suggestions and much encouragement as she reviewed the manuscript. Deborah Reidy, Neil Lazzara, and Lynn Ahlgrim-Delzell also offered helpful ideas.

I am grateful to the University of North Carolina at Charlotte and Dean Schley Lyons for providing me with a semester of leave from teaching so that I could write. Frances Canter was a great supporter as she eagerly contributed countless hours to typing manuscripts. Many others helped track down important documents, including Frada Mozenter, Dawn Hubbs, Nissa Coombs, Tracey Hoback, and Roz Kincaid. Others gave valuable support and encouragement as well, including Jim Conroy, Bill Covington, Dwayne Smith, Elise Fullmer, and Phyllis Mills. My wife, Joanna, was always patient and supportive when I needed time away from our relationship to write and she helped with important editing.

CONTENTS

Questions to Consider in Detecting Stigma for Readers, Labeled People and Agency Providers

CONFRONTING THE STIGMA
IN THEIR LIVES

Part I
LIVING WITH STIGMA

Chapter 1

INTRODUCTION: SO HOW SHOULD I REFER TO THE PEOPLE WHO ARE THE FOCUS OF THIS BOOK?

James: What will be the title of your book? Don't put down 'How a retarded person is.' Don't put the title down like that.

As I begin this book, I feel compelled to raise an important question— How will I refer to the people that it is about? This is a critical question because the language that we use can be a powerful form of stigma.

All of us who are involved or familiar with the field of developmental disabilities know that *how* we refer to people with a mental retardation label is important. The terms that we use can be very damaging. For example, just recalling that "moron," "idiot," and "imbecile" were once acceptable diagnostic categories should be warning enough. Today, all three of these grossly demeaning terms are among the worst to be used in hostile name-calling.

An attempt to improve upon these wretched diagnostic categories led to the introduction of "mental deficiency," but the term, "deficiency," has also became pejorative over time. More recently, that label has been replaced by "mental retardation," still a familiar and fairly acceptable diagnostic term to most people.

One recent effort to further humanize these diagnostic categories has been to use a broader term, "developmental disabilities." Developmental disabilities comprises several groups, including people labeled with mental retardation, people with autism, people with epilepsy, and others if they have a disability that significantly limits them in major areas of daily functioning.

So far, "developmental disabilities" seems less pejorative than "mental retardation." Combining people labeled with mental retardation with other groups has been a good strategy in that it has diffused the stigma associated with each of these individual groups. A disadvantage, however, is that the new label comprises an even more heterogeneous population, which further complicates program planning and fund raising efforts. Also by combining these groups, each one passes on its stigmatizing status to the others.

"Developmental disabilities" may only need more time before it becomes a stigmatizing term. Indeed, every new diagnostic term that is used to identify a stigmatic group of people is destined for eventual disposal. We will always need to be vigilant in our choice of terms, and we must involve the people who are labeled in these decisions.

People First

For over a decade, the self-advocacy movement has reminded us that the people identified by these diagnostic categories are "People First." The People First Movement has taught us to put "people" before a diagnosis to remind us of that we are all from the same human family (Edwards, 1982). In response to this movement's wishes, the most acceptable term that is currently used in many professional circles, including the American Association on Mental Retardation, is "people with mental retardation."

Yet, as improved as "people with mental retardation" is compared to previous terms, there are two problems with it. First, "mental retardation" is not one disease or medical condition as this term suggests. For example, people with arthritis or epilepsy bring to mind people having a particular physiological condition. In contrast, mental retardation brings to mind over 250 known etiologies. Downs syndrome, PKU (phenylketonuria), maternal diseases, hypoxia (lack of oxygen at birth), and childhood accidents are a few examples. "Mental retardation" is actually an **umbrella label** comprising a wide range of physiological and mental conditions, and it does not adequately communicate the diversity of conditions of the people with this label.

Furthermore, many people with a mental retardation label, particularly at the mild level, do not have an identifiable medical cause for their cognitive condition. People labeled with mild levels of retardation (as opposed to moderate, severe, and profound levels) are by far the largest subgroup with this label. They are often referred to as having "social retardation" or an environmentally-based form of cognitive impairment.

Environmental causes, while not directly proven, are thought to include poverty, poor nutrition, inadequate parenting, low quality formal education, inadequate housing, inadequate health care, and racism.

"Mental retardation" is a socially constructed label, and labels are assigned to people based on the definitions used by those assigning these labels. Therefore, probably the most accurate terminology that could be used is "people who are labeled with mental retardation" or "people who have a mental retardation label."

The second reason why I have problems with using "people with mental retardation" is that many people who have been referred to in this way dislike or even disavow being "mentally retarded" (e.g., Dudley, 1983; Edgerton, 1984; Edwards, 1982). Based on my respect for these concerns of some people, I will not use the term "mental retardation" without referring to it as a label. I believe that using this term in any other way in a book on stigma would be counterproductive. It would also be a betrayal of the people that the book is about.

I have decided to use the term, **"people"** in instances when it is self-evident who I am discussing. At other times, I use the phrases, **"people who are labeled with mental retardation"** or a more abbreviated term, **"labeled people."**

In *Living with Stigma,* I made a special effort to avoid referring to people as "the mentally retarded" or even "people with mental retardation." Yet, my review of that book painfully reminds me that I sometimes used "mental retardation" without identifying it as a label. I found it awkward to continually use "people first" and labeling language. I am more committed to appropriate terminology in this book because I know now more than before that this label is stigmatic to many people. Most important, using appropriate language is consistent with the ultimate purpose of this book, which is to bring greater respect to this particular group of people.

A Brief Glossary

The people who are the focus of this book are adults who are labeled with mental retardation. They are referred to as

"people"
"labeled people," or
"people who are labeled with mental retardation."

The term **"consumer"** is used when referring to this group of people when they are in the role of service recipients of the mental retardation system. Also, the mental retardation system is sometimes abbreviated as **"System"** with a capital "S."

Chapter 2

THE SIGNIFICANCE OF STIGMA

A New York consumer: We must change basic attitudes that our society has toward people with disabilities. Societal prejudice is one of the major obstacles preventing the independence and integration of people with disabilities (Jaskulski, Metzler, & Zierman, 1990, p. 198).

Paul: When my girlfriend, Bev, and I are in her neighborhood, walking down the street, the kids there say, "Look, here comes the retardate." Then they call Bev a retardate too. I tell them they are dummies. Actually, names can never hurt me, only stick and stones. I go and tell their parents and they side with their kids. So I go get a policeman to stop it (Dudley, 1983).

Paul, quoted above, is a 44-year-old man who is labeled with mental retardation and cerebral palsy. He walks with a noticeable limp and speaks with an obtrusive drawl. He has lived his entire life with his parents and now works as a kitchen helper, after working many years in a sheltered workshop.

Paul illustrates a problem that many labeled people experience. It is the problem of stigma that inevitably accompanies them wherever they go. They live within a complex web of social encounters that are tainted with stigma. Unfortunately, this problem has often forced them to live a confined, segregated existence. Helping them to confront the stigma in their lives and to break out of their segregated existence are the central purposes of this book.

Stigma is to people with a mental retardation label what racism is to African Americans and other ethnic minority groups. Stigma, like racism, is pervasive and endemic to their existence. Stigma restricts the stigmatized group's opportunities to succeed and thwarts their efforts to become more normalized. Stigma is manifested as an invisible veil that divides the stigmatized group from the opportunities and material resources taken for granted by the mainstream. And stigma like racism is so omnipresent that it is presumed by most people to be the only reality available in our society.

Neither stigma nor racism can be erased or eliminated in one generation, for they have existed and been perpetuated for centuries. Yet, this book brings a message of hope. Major efforts in confronting stigma have already begun to occur and must be intensified in the years ahead!

Disability Problems Versus Stigma Problems

Some key concepts in understanding the problem of stigma provide a common thread throughout the book. Two central concepts are "disability problems" and "stigma problems." These two concepts represent fundamentally different types of problems that need to be distinguished and overcome in different ways. Brief definitions are offered below.

Disability-Related Problems: "Disability-related problems" have their origins and are inherent in the person's disability. Every person who is labeled with mental retardation is presumed to have some form of cognitive limitation, determined by intelligence tests and/or adaptive behavior scales. Indeed, their cognitive limitations do, to varying degrees, limit or complicate their communication processes, employability, interpersonal relations, mobility, and capacity for self-sufficiency.

However, these disabilities vary in nature and severity in numerous ways (Jaskulski, Lakin, & Zierman, 1995). Some disabilities are minor and others are quite severe. Some people are slower in responding to ideas or lack a capacity for abstraction; others think quickly and are acutely analytic. One labeled person may have no capacity to operate a computer, for example, while another may be a computer whiz.

Stigma Problems: The stigma that is associated with a person's disability is the other type of problem impeding them from having a more normalized life. The concept of stigma, according to Goffman (1963), refers to stereotypes and myths that others project onto a person's attribute (or disability) when that attribute is considered both different from and inferior to societal norms. An updated definition of stigma adds an important condition—stigma leads to restrictions on the person's ability to develop his or her potential (Coleman, 1986). Stigma problems have their origins in society, not in the attributes of the person.

A peculiar characteristic of stigma is that people become aware of the specific discrediting attribute and subconsciously associate it with general stereotypes that they have learned. In the case of people labeled with mental retardation, other people become aware of their cognitive disability and often, without conscious thought, link the person with particular stereotypes. Examples include: they can not think or speak very well, they are incapable of working in the competitive world, and they are childlike and in need of protection.

These two concepts, disability-related problems and stigma problems, are both important, suggesting the need for a dual perspective. In examining a problem, we should consider the possibility that the problem has its origins in the individuals who have disabilities, other people and larger social units in the environment, or both.

The goal of self-determination illustrates the need for a dual perspective. If people lack self-determination, is this the result of a limitation inherent in their disability or a problem of stigma? It is quite feasible that it could be both. For example, some aspects of a cognitive disability may hinder analytic or problem-solving capabilities. Equally compelling, past and current practices of other people and groups may be barriers to self-determination because they have not provided adequate opportunities for labeled people to assume responsibility for themselves.

Disability-related problems are a central focus of the service provisions of the mental retardation system. Service providers or caregivers are trained to teach, socialize, and habilitate people to both overcome and compensate for many of their disability-related problems. In contrast, the stigma problems of people are given only minor or even superficial attention by the mental retardation system.

What Is the Problem?

Millions of people with mental retardation labels live in communities throughout the United States. Many have been previously institutionalized in mental retardation facilities, but most have always lived in the community.

Most of the people with these labels are dependent, to some degree, on the national deinstitutionalization movement that has returned tens of thousands of citizens from institutions to residential communities. This movement began in the 1960's, ignited by a period of reform and optimism. Since this time, an extensive array of community-based services have been established in residential care, employment, health care, mental health treatment, recreation, and leisure.

The deinstitutionalization movement was a long overdue response to a previously forgotten segment of our population. Indeed, it is an affirmation of their humanity and a mandate for them to rightfully claim full citizenship in society. This movement has brought many individuals unprecedented freedom, opportunity, and access to a more normalized life. It offers a radical departure from the previous institutional era that existed for over a century and fostered isolation, regimentation, and dependency.

This movement has had major success in physically integrating people labeled with mental retardation into the community. Most living arrangements, some employment sites and training centers, and many recreational activities are typically located in normalized physical structures, weaved into the communities where all people live, work, and play.

Moreover, the mental retardation system continues to be reasonably successful in preparing its consumers with skills and competencies to participate with some degree of independence and self-sufficiency in this normalized world. Those who use services typically develop skills in hygiene and self-care, work-related tasks, basic communication, managing their households, and transportation.

The deinstitutionalization movement has needed a philosophy to guide it, and "normalization" has been the dominant philosophy in the past. Normalization theory has inculcated the value that all people with disabilities should have the opportunity to live their lives as culturally similar to others as their disability allows (Brown & Smith, 1992; Flynn & Nitsch, 1980; Wolfensberger, 1972). Among other things, normalization refers to a normal life experience, including having friends, being employed, and contributing to society. Normalization also means having opportunities to develop intimate relationships. It means having economic needs, opportunities, and securities. It also refers to living in an ordinary home and community. In a fundamental sense, normalization philosophy infers that the lives of people with cognitive disabilities are as important as the lives of other citizens.

The ambiguities involved in defining a "normalized" environment and the challenges to implementing such an ideal have led to alternative goals as well. The "least restricted alternative" is one example (Turnbull, Ellis, Boggs, Brooks, & Biklen, 1981). This concept offers a less complicated set of criteria than normalization for designing residential services, habilitation plans, and support services. The least restricted alternative has also been used in court decisions to clarify that labeled people have a Constitutional right to protection from "undue restraint."

Wolfensberger (1983) has crafted another helpful concept, "social role valorization," for guiding the design of service provisions. Creating and supporting socially valued roles for people within the community is highly desired in such areas as employment, family relationships, household management, and community activities. This emphasis on valued roles is particularly important because of the pervasive harm of past and current devalued roles assigned to people.

While "normalization," "least restricted environment," "social role valorization," and other conceptualizations are helpful in articulating the *goals* of deinstitutionalization, conceptualizations of the *problem definition* have not been given as much serious attention. For example, what is the nature of the problem(s) that these three concepts (normalization, least restrictive alternative, and social role valorization) are attempting to solve?

The concept of stigma is helpful in expanding our understanding of the nature of the overall "problem" faced by the deinstitutionalization movement. Both stigma problems and disability-related problems must be addressed. Disability-related problems are inherent in the disabilities of labeled people, and stigma problems are inherent in societal conditions. The very different origins of these problems require two very different problem-solving approaches. Both problems must be confronted if success is to be the ultimate outcome of this movement.

Intelligence, Attractiveness, and Self-Sufficiency

Stigma is a cultural phenomenon that varies from one society to another (Becker & Arnold, 1986). Postindustrialized, Western societies, like the United States, have values that seem to foster greater stigma toward people with a mental retardation label than other societies. Three societal values in particular are instinctively treasured — intelligence, physical attractiveness, and self-sufficiency — and labeled people often are lacking in all three of them.

Intelligence: Our postindustrialized, computer-age economy is arranged to financially and socially benefit people with higher intelligence. People who can understand the complexities of the social order and are capable of manipulating it have the greatest opportunities to succeed. Jobs are increasingly being stratified by intelligence, with workers at the lower levels relying on the intelligence and direction of the people above them. People with higher levels of intelligence continue to move up, and people with lower intelligence remain at the bottom rungs.

Attractiveness: Our society is also obsessed with physical beauty, exhibited for us by movie and TV stars, and fashion models. Physical attractiveness is prized and promoted all around us by the media; it is prominently displayed in women's and men's magazines, mail catalogs, TV programs, movies, on billboards, and in the public images of most professional people. This value adds up to a sad reality for the people that our society has defined as less physically attractive, particularly those with unattractive facial features, unusual body sizes and proportions, unfashionable clothing and hair styles, and those with inaccessibility to the resources that promote beauty.

Self-sufficiency: Self-sufficiency is also an admired quality in our society and one that is becoming even more important in recent political debates. Being able to take care of your family and yourself is increasingly becoming a bottom-line measure of your social respectability. Those that need special assistance or help, whether it is financial, medical care, subsidized housing, or habilitation services, are assumed to be residual and less respectable.

High intelligence, physical attractiveness, and self-sufficiency are among the most admired qualities in the United States, and people who are labeled with mental retardation are usually not well endowed with them. By internalizing these three general qualities as basic to our being, we have been forced into a mind set that devalues most labeled people. Possibly, we devalue them more than any other group in society because they do not score high in intelligence, beauty, and self-reliance.

Progress in Societal Inclusion?

In *Living with Stigma*, I stated that the social dimension of the normalized world was the next frontier for the deinstitutionalization movement. My assessment at that time was that relatively little had been accomplished in integrating labeled people into the social fabric of their communities.

The interpersonal relationships of the people whom I studied in 1983 seemed largely restricted to other consumers and staff members within the mental retardation system, with relatively few having meaningful associations with neighbors, other employees, club and church members, and friends from other places in the community.

I also observed that most of them were employed in day programs and sheltered workshops that were segregated from the mainstream. Their leisure was also mostly confined to activities involving other people with disabilities, such as special dances and community events like ball games. Also, many were frequenting restaurants and movie theaters in small groups on their own. I concluded in 1983 that social integration was minimal at best.

How much farther along is social integration or inclusion as we approach the 21st century? My impressions are that considerable progress has been made in some areas and very little in others. The indications of progress are readily evident. The policies and program initiatives of many community-based mental retardation programs reveal some of this progress. Supported employment and supported living programs are among the best program initiatives, even though they are still offered to only a small fraction of eligible individuals.

Supported employment programs have become one alternative to sheltered workshops. These programs have successfully prepared growing numbers of people with the skills, supports, and self-confidence needed to work in normal settings like hospitals, fast food restaurants, factories, and grocery stores. Job coaches are among their partners who assist and support them on the job.

Similarly, supported living programs offer a more individualized and normalized home environment for people (O'Brien, 1994). Decisions about where people live are based on their needs and preferences. The home is owned by the consumer or a landlord; it is not a service facility run by the System. Also other natural supports are provided in the community.

Besides these exceptional program initiatives, other indicators of progress are also evident. The self-advocacy movement has mushroomed nationwide over the last 15 years and seems much stronger both in numbers of participants and power (Longhurst, 1994). Further, emerging leaders of the self-advocacy movement are beginning to be taken more seriously as consultants and decision-makers about the needs of labeled people.

Some exemplary community education agencies are also becoming more evident in the movement. These agencies have promulgated new philosophical perspectives, training modules, and services to address the prejudices and organizational barriers to normalized living. Community integration projects, school-age projects emphasizing integration, and community transition projects are examples (Consortium Annual Report, 1994).

All of these initiatives are among the most effective known means of eradicating stigma, and it is imperative that they continue to be funded and supported. However, despite these many hopeful new initiatives and developments, my judgment is that the lives of labeled people are far from being socially inclusive.

Public Polls on Disability Attitudes

Public opinion polls offer one indication of the extent of progress made in overcoming stigma in recent years. Public attitudes were quite positive as far back as the 1970s. A Gallup Poll back in 1976 suggested that attitudes toward people labeled with mental retardation were relatively positive. According to that poll, 85 percent of those interviewed said that they would not object to "six mentally retarded people occupying a home on their block." Also, 74 percent of those polled indicated that they did not fear people who had mental retardation labels.

In 1991, Louis Harris and Associates conducted another poll on public attitudes toward people with disabilities (Harris, 1991). This poll focused on all types of disabilities, not just mental retardation. Ninety-eight percent of those polled believed that people with disabilities should have an equal opportunity to participate in American society, and 90 percent believed that the society would benefit if these individuals would become more productive and contributing to the economy.

This Harris poll also reveals that the public has considerable exposure to people with disabilities in general. When asked if they knew anyone with a disability, 55 percent indicated that they had a friend with a disability, 28 percent knew a neighbor, and 22 percent had a member of their household. Further, 32 percent indicated that they had a "close friend or relative" with a disability.

However, a set of stigma-related questions was also asked by the Harris Poll (1991) that raise a red flag about public opinions toward people with disabilities in general. Seventy-five percent of the people polled reported feeling "pity" for people with a serious disability, 60 percent reported feeling "awkward or embarrassed" around such people, and 46 percent expressed "fear."

Another recent national poll focused on both mental retardation and mental illness and also raised concern about stigma issues. The Daniel Yankelovich Group (1989) found that 23 percent of those surveyed "absolutely would not welcome" people with mental disabilities into their neighborhoods. Another 29 percent would be reluctant to welcome them. Sixty percent admitted that they should know "a good deal more" about mental retardation.

One could conclude from these polls that public attitudes are improving in some ways and not in others. Larger numbers of people are having contact with people with disabilities in recent years and almost all are favorable to giving them equal opportunities. However, stereotypes also seem to be evident in many people's feelings toward labeled people and in their views about where they should live.

Research Studies of Labeled People

Progress in societal inclusion can also be assessed by considering the views of labeled people in research studies. Two very different studies provide a sampling of such views. These studies are Edgerton's 30-year longitudinal study and a recent national consumer study on self-determination.

Edgerton's Longitudinal Study: This classic longitudinal study on the problems of stigma is an important one to consider. Edgerton's *Cloak of Competence* (1967, 1993), first conducted during 1960–61, was an ethnographic study that initially conceptualized and described the problem of stigma for people labeled with mental retardation. The study sampled 48 adults who were labeled mildly retarded and had recently been discharged from a large mental retardation institution in California.

Edgerton found that their problems of daily living, while critical, were less serious than problems related to stigma. Entering the world outside the hospital involved a "bewildering array of demands for competence." Edgerton's subjects faced two related problems: denying to themselves that they were "mentally retarded," and passing, so that others neither suspected nor accused them of being "retarded."

This study also revealed that almost all of the subjects were dependent to some degree on "benefactors," including employers, spouses, lovers, close relatives, landladies, and neighbors who helped them with their problems. These benefactors not only assisted the subjects with practical problems but also with passing and denial efforts. Edgerton concluded this stage of his study by stating that the "benevolent conspiracy" of benefactors protecting these citizens had been most significant in helping them maintain themselves in the community. Otherwise, it was doubtful that most of them would have survived outside an institution.

In 1971–72, Edgerton and Bercovici (1976) conducted a 10-year follow-up study of thirty persons from the original sample. Concerns with stigma and passing were found to be far less evident. Benefactors played either the same or a less important role than before. Most of the people said that they were happier or things were about the same as they were ten years before.

Again, two decades later, Edgerton, Bollinger, and Herr (1984) studied 15 of the original cohort who could be found. Overall, these people were found to be less dependent upon others, particularly "benefactors." Some of the subjects still used passing techniques. For example, one man who could never read said, "I can't make that out. I'm getting old."

Almost three decades after the original study, the lives of six of the people in Edgerton's were reported on again (Edgerton and Gaston, 1991). Like before, these older adults were surviving and living fairly normal lives, with all but one having meaningful, long-term intimate relationships and other friends. They were less concerned about the stigma of institutionalization and being labeled mentally retarded. They were no longer heavily relying on benefactors; now most of them were in the role of helping others. Significantly, they were not active consumers of the mental retardation system. The authors concluded that these relatively independent people seemed better off and less helpless than people of similar age and IQ who lived in more restricted residential settings sponsored by the System.

One could generalize from this longitudinal study a statement of hope. These labeled people eventually become integrated into the social fabric of society; integration, however, followed a long journey of struggles and required the supports of all kinds of people.

National Self-Determination Study: Another study relevant to stigma was conducted on self-determination (Wehmeyer & Metzler, 1995). This national survey of 4544 labeled individuals asked whether they participated in the choices determining their lives, such as where they live, their job, friends, and how to spend their money. Also, they were asked how often they frequented socially integrated activities in the community. While this study was not longitudinal, the results offer understanding of the significance of stigma in the nineties.

The study concluded that the subjects were not very self-determining. Educational and home environments seemed overly protective and structured. Choices were available to people in some of the minor areas such as the clothes that they would wear and the choice of their leisure activities. Yet, they were not very involved in the more important decisions about their lives such as selecting a roommate, choosing where they lived, and influencing the people who were hired to serve them.

In addition, degrees of decision-making were often overlooked, as "all or nothing" seemed to be the pattern. For example, people were either able to attend an outing to a mall, movie, or sports event with a group of peers, or they did not have an outing at all. In addition, many felt that they were not engaging in activities and roles for adults, like getting married, receiving a decent wage, or owning a home.

One major theme identified in both of the above studies is an irony that should be faced. The community mental retardation system can be a formidable obstacle to independence, self-determination, and happiness rather than the catalyst that it should be. Further, this book reveals that the System can be a major perpetrator of stigma.

Diversity Issues and Stigma

Stigma associated with disabilities is manifested differently across various ethnic communities in American society. Generally, stigma seems to be less problematic in minority communities than white communities. While few studies have focused on ethnic diversity and stigma, three pertinent studies are summarized below to highlight some diversity issues.

Chicano Study: An in-depth interview study by Henshel (1972) compared labeled people who were Anglos and Chicanos. Henshel concluded that IQ scores were less significant in determining the life patterns of the subjects than their ethnicity. The Chicano subjects evaluated themselves more positively than the Anglos, although they seemed more frequently plagued with adversity. Generally they led more normal lives according to the standards of their subculture because they received more support from their own ethnic group through extended kinship and friendship networks.

The Chicanos dated considerably more than their Anglo counterparts and had more close companions with whom they shared recreational pursuits. While the contacts that all of the subjects had with neighbors were limited, the Chicanos tended to have more neighbors with whom they were in contact, and their frequency of contact was greater than that of the Anglos. Henshel concluded that their supportive kinship and friendship networks were more accepting of mental retardation.

Living with Stigma: My study also revealed differences in stigma based on the ethnicity of the subjects and their neighborhoods (Dudley, 1983). The subjects who resided in a working class, African American neighborhood seemed to have less awareness and concern about stigma than subjects in the three middle class neighborhoods. All but one of the six subjects living in the working class neighborhood were African American. The neighbors were noticeably more positive in their interaction with these subjects than neighbors in the other three communities. For example, the researchers observed that the subjects were often warmly greeted, at times they were embraced or hugged, and occasionally they were invited to neighborhood events like cook-outs.

Koegel and Edgerton Study: Another study focused on 45 African American young adults who were thought to be "six-hour retarded children" during their school years (Koegel & Edgerton, 1982). "Six-hour retarded children" are typically labeled "mildly retarded" and attend special classes during their school hours but are supposedly viewed as "normal" at home and in their neighborhoods. Large numbers of people from low income backgrounds qualify as "six-hour retarded children," but little is known about their lives outside the schools and later in their lives.

This ethnographic study sheds some light on people referred to as "six-hour retarded children." The study revealed that the subjects actually did not "disappear" into their community as "normal people." They were viewed by their family members and others as "slow" and having adaptation problems. Most of the subjects also applied labels to themselves that acknowledged intellectual limitations. They acknowledged having problems with reading and writing, counting, self-maintenance, and vocational pursuits. Also, as adults they experienced difficulties in their social relationships, self-esteem, judgement and understanding, vulnerability to exploitation, and parenting roles.

This study points out that low income, African American communities may reject the labels used by the mental retardation system and schools, but they are well aware of the intellectual impairments of their labeled members. The greatest differences may be in their expectations. These communities appeared to offer labeled people many integrative experiences with nondisabled people and to encourage them to take on normal roles, such as having a family and their own children.

Based on these three studies, the stigma of labeled people from lower income and minority groups may be considered less problematic within their own cultures. However, they still must confront the stigma that exists in the larger society and within the mental retardation system.

Diversity issues related to ethnicity and race will be identified and examined again in later chapters.

Taking a Personal Inventory on Stigma

I believe that we should continually be involved in a process of examining and changing *ourselves* as part of our effort to confront stigma. Stigma is a social problem that is so pervasive that we can be unaware of its impact on us. At this early point in the book, it may be helpful for you, the reader, to take a personal inventory of your attitudes toward stigma. The following exploratory questions may help you to detect some of your personal biases and stereotypes.

1. What thoughts and feelings do you have when you hear the term, "mental retardation"?
2. Are there ways that you promote stigma toward labeled people?
3. Do you have any close friends who are labeled with mental retardation? If not, why do you think that this is so?
4. Can you easily identify some of the strengths of labeled people that you know fairly well? If not, why do you think that this is so?
5. If you work in the developmental disabilities field, what motivated you to work with this particular group? Are you aware of any feelings of pity or guilt that have influenced you?

References

Brown, H., & Smith, H. (Eds.) (1992). *Normalisation: A reader for the nineties.* New York: Tavistock/Routledge.

Becker, G., & Arnold, R. (1986). Stigma as a social and cultural construct. In S. Ainlay, G. Becker, & L. Coleman (Eds.), *The dilemma of difference: A multidisciplinary view of stigma.* New York: Plenum.

Coleman, L. (1986). Stigma: An enigma demystified. In S. Ainlay, G. Becker, & L. Coleman (Eds.), *The dilemma of difference: A multidisciplinary view of stigma.* New York: Plenum.

Consortium Annual Report (1994). The Consortium Annual Report, FY 1993–1994, Holyoke, MA.

Daniel Yankelovich Group. (1989). Public opinion poll on chronic mental illness, Roper Center for Public Opinion Research, File 468.

Dudley, J. (1983). *Living with stigma: The plight of the people who we label mentally retarded.* Springfield, IL: Charles C Thomas.

Edgerton, R. (1967). *Cloak of competence: Stigma in the lives of the mentally retarded.* Los Angeles: University of California Press.

Edgerton, R. (1993). *Cloak of competence: Stigma in the lives of the mentally retarded, Revised and Updated.* Los Angeles: University of California Press.

Edgerton, R., & Bercovici, S. (1976). The cloak of competence: Years later. *American Journal of Mental Deficiency, 80*(5), 485–497.

Edgerton, R., Bollinger, M., & Herr, B. (1984). The cloak of competence: After two decades. *American Journal on Mental Deficiency, 88*(4), 345–351.

Edgerton, R., & Gaston, (Eds.) (1991). *I've seen it all!: Lives of older persons with mental retardation in the community.* Baltimore: Paul H. Brookes.

Flynn, R., & Nitsch, K. (1980). *Normalization, social integration, and community services.* Baltimore: University Park Press.

Gallup Poll (1976). Gallup Organization Report for the President's Committee on Mental Retardation: Public attitudes regarding mental retardation. In R. Nathan (ed.), *Mental retardation: Century of decision.* Washington, D.C.: U. S. Government Printing Office, 1976.

Goffman, E. (1963). *Stigma: Notes on the management of spoiled identity.* Engelwood Cliffs, NJ: Prentice-Hall.

Harris, L. and Associates. (1991). Public attitudes toward people with disabilities. Study Number 912028.

Henshel, A. (1972). *The forgotten ones: A sociological study of Anglo and Chicano retardates.* Austin: University of Texas Press.

Jaskulski, T., Lakin, K., & Zierman, S. (1995). *The journey to inclusion: A resource guide for state policymakers.* Washington, D.C.: President's Committee on Mental Retardation.

Jaskulski, T., Metzler, C., & Zierman, S. (1990). *The 1990 reports: Forging a new era.* Washington, D.C.: National Association of Developmental Disabilities Council, May, 1990.

Koegel, P., & Edgerton, R. (1982). Labeling and the perception of handicap among black mildly mentally retarded adults. *American Journal of Mental Deficiency, 87*(3), 266–276.

Longhurst, N. (1994). *The self-advocacy movement by people with developmental disabilities: A demographic study and directory of self-advocacy groups in the United States.* Washington, D.C.: American Association on Mental Retardation.

O'Brien, J. (1994). Down stairs that are never your own: Supporting people with developmental disabilities in their own homes. *Mental Retardation, 32*(1), 1–6.

Turnbull, H., Ellis, J., Boggs, E., Brooks, P., & Biklen, D. (1981): *The least restrictive alternative: Principles and practices.* Washington, D.C.: American Association on Mental Retardation.

Wehmeyer, M., & Metzler, C. (1995). How self-determined are people with mental retardation? The national consumer survey. *Mental Retardation, 33*(2), 111–119.

Wolfensberger, W. (1972). *The principle of normalization in human services.* Toronto: National Institute on Mental Retardation.

Wolfensberger, W. (1983). Social role valorization: A proposed new term for the principle of normalization. *Mental Retardation, 21*(6), 234–239.

Chapter 3

THE PROMOTION OF STIGMA

Mary: When visitors come into my (sheltered workshop) to see what is going on, they come up to me and say, 'What are you doing?' when it is obvious. I tell them, but I want to say 'What do you think I'm doing?' (Dudley, 1983)!

A Maine consumer: I want to work for the same reason other people want to work, which is to support myself and to feel like part of the world. Why is that so hard for people to understand (Jaskulski, Metzler, & Zierman, 1990, p. 72).

Phillip: When are you guys going to wise up? You got to know what you're doing. You wouldn't treat yourselves that way (Dudley, 1983).

Most people are likely to have only a partial or superficial understanding of stigma and how it is promoted. The word "stigma" may evoke dramatic images, like a cruel act of sexual abuse against a defenseless disabled person, or a violent expression of outrage by alarmed residents against people with disabilities moving into their neighborhood. In reality, stigma-promotion can be manifested in a wide variety of forms and degrees of severity. It can also involve a range of people and social groups as perpetrators, including friends and family members as well as acquaintances and strangers.

A stigma is an "undesired differentness" of a person that leads to restrictions on the person's physical and social mobility and access to opportunities for developing his or her potential (Coleman, 1986). Stigma is a concept that has meaning for many groups, not just people with disabilities. According to Goffman (1963), the concept of stigma can be helpful in explaining the problems confronting three general categories of people. Stigma can be associated with racial, ethnic, or religious identity. Stigma can be associated with behavior patterns that are contrary to societal norms. Examples include homosexuality and alcoholism. Finally, stigma can be associated with deformities of the body, the category in which a person labeled with mental retardation would most naturally fit.

Stigma has its origins in the values, attitudes, and cognitive processes of a society and in countless people and social groups. Stigma becomes manifested when contact occurs between labeled people and those who promote it. As Goffman (1963) points out, the encounters between the stigmatized and "normals" reveal the immediate causes and the effects of stigma.

The Process of Stigma-Promotion

Stigma-promoting processes (1) have their origins in fears, socialization, and social control mechanisms; (2) these origins lead to the promulgation of stereotypes and myths about labeled people; and (3) these stereotypes and myths are used to promote acts of stigma.

1. Origins of Stigma: We still have only a partial understanding of the origins of stigma. Many theories provide explanations. Stigma has its origins in people who serve as references or mentors for us (Coleman, 1986). As part of our socialization, we look to someone else's understanding to help form our own. Our parents, teachers, and later influential figures informally teach us, among other things, stereotypes and how to identify stigmatized groups. Stereotypes and myths about stigmatized people are thought to be aspects of "cultural wisdom" that are transmitted from one generation to the next through socialization (Crocker & Lutsky, 1986). Young children, for example, may hear derogatory comments or testimonies of pity about a labeled person from family members, teachers, or peers. If these children have no direct opportunities to become acquainted with labeled people, they are likely to construct their understanding largely from these messages. Children can also learn these stereotypes from books, TV programs, and other agents of society.

Stigma also often originates in people's feelings, such as dislikes, distrust, and disgust (Coleman, 1986). Fears in particular are instrumental in perpetuating stigma, including the fears of differences in people and the fears about the unknown etiology of an undesirable attribute. Stigmatizing others brings a sense of safety, predictability, and order to things. For example, believing that other people deserve or bring onto themselves their misfortune is reassuring that it will not happen to us. Or some people may need to feel good about themselves and have to "put others down" to elevate themselves.

Various forms of social control are also responsible for the perpetuation of stigma. The controls imposed by social units like schools, neighborhood groups, social agencies, companies, and other systems reinforce social norms including those that are stigmatizing. Neighborhood groups, for example, partially exist to promote rising residential property values, and "undesirable" newcomers are kept out of neighborhoods to accomplish this goal. Also, groups of people are stigmatized and exploited to preserve larger social structures. For example, our capitalist economy always needs people without skills to do menial work for minimum wages (Crocker & Lutsky, 1986).

2. Promulgating Stereotypes and Myths About Groups of People: Based on an assumption that people with disabilities are not fully human, an ideology of stigma gets constructed and promulgated in society to explain their inferiority (Goffman, 1963). This ideology is comprised of numerous negative stereotypes and myths about this group. According to the *Random House Dictionary*, "stereotypes" are simplified and standardized conceptions of particular groups of people that are invested with special meaning. A "myth" is something imaginary or fictitious. It can also be an unproved collective belief that is accepted uncritically and is used to justify a social institution. Both stereotypes and myths foster the notion that everyone in a particular group is essentially alike, rather than understanding people as individuals with unique characteristics.

Stereotypes and myths provide us with social constructions of how to perceive labeled people. These constructions are then used to inform our individual behavior and organizational practices that are demeaning and detrimental to labeled people.

People rely on these stereotypes and myths, particularly if they have little access to accurate information about disabilities. Also, these stereotypes and myths become more deeply ingrained when people do not have opportunities to develop close associations and friendships with labeled people. Goffman (1963) states that we lean on these incorrect understandings about people until they become transformed into "normative expectations" or even "righteously presented demands."

Furthermore, stereotypes and myths can easily multiply in meaning. According to Goffman, as uninformed people draw on myths associated with one stigmatized group, they combine these myths with those associated with other stigmatized groups and make sweeping generalizations about stigmatized groups in general. What happens is that we assign or impute a wide range of imperfections onto people with disabilities based on the original perceived imperfection, their cognitive disability (Goffman, 1963). For example, we may see someone who has limited cognitive skills and we presume that they have limited feelings and sexual desires as well.

Individuals and social groups in our society hold many popular stereotypes and myths about people with a mental retardation label that are destructive. Some of the more familiar stereotypes and myths are presented below as examples (partly based on Wolfensberger, 1976). All of these examples have been challenged and proven to be either over-generalizations or false.

Some stereotypes and myths refer to misconceptions about the mental retardation label, for example:

- Mental retardation is a fixed condition that cannot be changed.
- Mental retardation is contagious.
- Labeled people have offsprings who also have mental retardation.

Other stereotypes and myths raise questions about their capabilities, for example:

- Labeled people cannot develop into mature adults.
- They do not have feelings like other people.
- They are sexually underdeveloped.
- They can be assaultive and destructive.
- They cannot effectively speak for themselves.
- They are not reliable subjects for research.
- They cannot become self-sufficient.
- They will lower the values of other residential properties where they live.
- They cannot manage or own a house.
- They cannot sustain a job in the regular work world.

3. Stigma-Promoting Acts Are the Outcome: Stigma-promoting acts derive directly from faulty perceptions about labeled people. *Stigma-promoting acts are defined in this book as acts involving others (individuals, groups, institutions) that are motivated by stereotypes and myths, and lead to restricting the opportunities of labeled people to develop their potential.*

One condition incorporated into the above definition is that the perpetrator is motivated by stereotypes or myths about the person's disability. In some cases, the motivation of the perpetrator is obvious (e.g., calling someone a "retard"). In instances when the perpetrator's motivation is not obvious, the person who is the object of the demeaning act becomes important in assessing whether or not it is stigma-promoting. In addition, an act can be stigma-promoting even if the person who is the object of the act does not perceive it this way. It is important to note that while most stigma-promoting acts do not have obvious or explicit motivations, many labeled people can keenly sense when the perpetrators are motivated by misconceptions about them.

Many of the types of stigma promotion presented below are problems peculiar to people with cognitive disabilities, while other types may be applicable to other devalued groups as well. In both instances, these acts are considered stigma-promoting. It is important to emphasize that the stigma problems of people with a mental retardation label are, at times, similar to those of other stigmatized groups of people.

Types of Stigma-Promotion

An exhaustive list of all existing types of stigma-promotion would be difficult to compile. The typology in Table 1 below, however, is intended to acquaint readers with some of the most common ones. Readers are encouraged to add other types of acts to this list based on your experiences. Most importantly, I hope that this typology will stimulate further discussion about this problem.

This typology has been developed primarily by consulting labeled people. The primary sources are qualitative studies of labeled people and various reports, newsletters, and books from the self-advocacy movement and its representatives. In most instances, illustrations of stigma-promotion are included to depict how these acts affect people on a personal level. The sources of illustrations are referenced except for those that have been taken from *Living with Stigma*.

This typology in Table 1 depicts stigma-promotion at many levels of social intercourse including the interpersonal, organizational, and institutional levels. The first four types could be evident on either the interpersonal or organizational/institutional level. The fifth type, "more extreme derogatory and abusive practices" is most likely manifested on an interpersonal level. The last two types are primarily organizational and institutional manifestations.

1. Inappropriate Use of Labels and Other Terms

In Chapter 1, I identified a basic concern of the book by asking the question, "How should I refer to the people who are the focus of this

Table 1
Types of Stigma-Promoting Acts

1. Inappropriate use of language and other terms
2. Communication that is age-inappropriate
3. Invasions of privacy
4. Other barriers to open communication
   A. Not allowing people to speak for themselves
   B. Ignoring communication
   C. Insensitivity to the characteristics of a person's disability
5. More extreme derogatory and abusive practices
   A. Staring
   B. Ridicule and blatant rejection
   C. Physical and sexual abuse
6. Other organizational and programmatic barriers
   A. Inappropriate restrictions
   B. Segregated programming
   C. Overlooking more valued roles
   D. Insensitivity to stigma identifiers
7. Other violations of civil and human rights

book?" The terminology that we use in our interpersonal and organizational communication is extremely important, as it can readily effect labeled people and their relationships with others.

Examples of words that are sometimes inappropriately used by people having close associations with labeled people are (Research & Training Center on Independent Living, 1990):

- "Handicap" ("disability" is currently a more appropriate term.)
- "The disabled" ("people with disabilities" is more appropriate.)
- Words like "unfortunate, pitiful, deaf, dumb, crippled, and deformed" are offensive.

Other examples include:

- "I got the pick of the litter (referring to new consumers discharged from an institution)."
- "You are a very capable little girl . . . I mean, grown woman."

Examples of inappropriate language used by acquaintances and strangers can be even harsher, for example:

- Words like "retard," "tard," "vegetable," and "dumb."
- "Look, here comes the retardate."
- "People where I work call me stupid."
- "No one would go out with you the way you look."

- "People in my neighborhood call me 'big lips' and 'You look like a truck rolled over you!' (said by a man with a cleft lip)."
- Frequent use of such terms as "moron," and "idiot" on TV shows (Stevens, 1996).

In many instances, the people who have associations with labeled people are unaware of a labeled individual's disdain for words like "retardate," "the mentally retarded," or even "people with mental retardation." Most labeled people, particularly those at the mild or moderate levels, are opposed to being referred to in this way (Dudley, 1983; Edgerton, 1984; Edwards, 1982; Jaskulski, Lakin, & Zierman, 1995). To them, these terms refer to a general debilitation of dependency and incompetence.

Most of the people who deny being mentally retarded do, however, admit to having a disability. They prefer to describe it as a specific learning deficiency such as being slow or having difficulty reading. Some prefer to emphasize the physical aspects of their disability, such as cerebral palsy, seizures, or a speech impediment. Overall, they prefer to view it as a localized condition rather than a more general debilitation (Dudley, 1983; Koegel & Edgerton, 1982; Lorber, 1974).

Referring to someone as "mentally retarded" may even be inappropriate for those who seem comfortable with the label, as it carries negative connotations that may thwart their strivings. For example, a staff member who perceives a consumer as "mentally retarded" will likely have difficulty setting aside stereotypes associated with the label to relate to the consumer as a unique individual.

Also, words that were appropriate in the past may be totally unacceptable today (e.g., moron). To be terminology-sensitive, we must periodically reconsider what is acceptable language, particularly from the perspectives of people with a label. No doubt the words that are currently acceptable will be discarded at some point in the future as no label has had a useful life indefinitely.

Labels may have utility in some instances, such as in obtaining funds for programs. However, when we use labels to refer to people, whether in their presence or not, they tend to transmit stereotypes that interfere with how we perceive and interact with them. Agencies are often insensitive to the preferences of their consumers and continue to include these labels on their stationary, on vans that transport their consumers, in public reports, and in conversations.

2. Communication that Is Age-Inappropriate

Many people subconsciously think of labeled adults as if they are children or teenagers. The manner in which we talk to them or nonverbally interact with them conveys this message. For example, the words "kids" and "children" are often mistakenly used in referring to adults.

The incidents below provide further examples of this problem:

- A friend of the family pinched Dora on the cheek. It was meant to be an expression of endearment but was perceived by Nora as "disgusting."
- A staff person patted Nancy on the head and shoulders and then talked to her "like a baby," according to Nancy, who was extremely embarrassed by this.
- "I have people come to me and talk to me, as if I'm a child or hard-of-hearing: '(they say) How are you?' You're a good boy'" (Williams & Shoultz, 1982, p. 78).
- Sometimes theater clerks allow a small adult to get into the movie theater for a children's fee (Stevens, 1996).

Also, many agencies continue to offer programs for adults that are more appropriate for children. Examples include children's games, songs, or cartoons; making Valentines Day cards; and visiting Santa at Christmas. An individual from the state of Washington provides another illustration: "Do you really think I like going to that summer camp for the disabled? I'm 40 years old! Hell, if I had the money . . . I'd go to Hawaii like everyone else" (Jaskulski et al., 1990, p. 88).

3. Invasions of Privacy

Confidentiality is a professional ethic that human service workers sometimes overlook. This ethical standard is excessively abused with labeled people. Confidentiality can be overlooked in different ways, for example:

- An incident involved a staff member who told a researcher, without solicitation, that one of her consumers had just begun having sexual relations with her boyfriend.
- An incident involved two staff members who entertained each other during dinner with personal information about two of the individuals using their services.
- A staff member who asked Paul a number of personal questions,

stressed that his responses would be kept strictly confidential, and then discussed his responses with Paul's parents.

Another common practice is for staff or family members to openly talk about a labeled person's private life in the person's presence, which can also be a public embarrassment. An example involved Ruth who said that the staff at her residence were talking to each other in great detail about two former residents. Ruth overheard them talking and said, "They talk with company about us and act like we don't hear them, but we do."

4. Other Barriers to Open Communication

Several other barriers to open interpersonal communication can also occur. Some of the major types reported by labeled people are not allowing them opportunities to speak for themselves, ignoring their communication, and being insensitive to the characteristics of their disability.

A. Not Allowing People to Speak for Themselves: Stigma is promoted when people are not encouraged to voice their views or concerns. It is most detrimental when their voices are not considered in decisions about their lives. Examples of discouraging or not allowing the person's self-expression are:

- Ron, who lived in a small group residence, was unexpectedly sent to another group home on a trial basis. He expressed anger about this because the "big shots" sent him without even asking him what he wanted. He was later assigned to another group home without his input even though he had told them of his displeasure.
- An Oklahoma consumer of residential services describes how he is left out of decisions: "I live in a group home with my roommate, but I have no choice. I want my own place and my own job. I am 57 years old. Another thing, my brother keeps all my money and I don't like that either. I think that I should have some choice in things" (Jaskulski et al., 1990, p. 105).
- Paul chose to withdraw from an agency activity because it reminded him of a traumatic experience that he had experienced as a teenager. Instead of asking Paul about this traumatic experience, the staff member called his sister for an explanation without informing him. Paul later said that he did not object to the call,

but he wanted the staff member to consult him first. This was also a violation of confidentiality.

- Mary who is in a wheelchair said that some staff have a habit of communicating with each other about her needs rather than talking directly to her. She feels like she doesn't even exist.
- Many people report that waitresses at restaurants overlook the labeled person when taking an order.

At times, the voices of these people are also overlooked in research studies even though this is becoming less of a problem. As one person put it, "Many opportunities can be created for people with disabilities to speak for themselves. I'm really glad they asked the people with a disability to fill out this survey instead of the parents and guardians like they usually do" (Jaskulski et al., 1990, p. 154).

A continuing tendency in the mental retardation field is for human service workers and family members to represent consumers when their needs are being considered. Too often, however, this benevolence is misguided and should be replaced by supporting, assisting, and teaching people to represent themselves. Often labeled people do not assume a significant role in case conferences that are convened for individual goal setting, evaluation of their performance, or considering changes in their programs. When their views are sought, the tendency is to downplay their significance presumably because it is not well articulated, may seem too simple, or is contrary to the viewpoints of others who have control.

B. Ignoring Communication: Disregarding or ignoring a labeled person's comments is another form of stigma-promotion when it is motivated by misconceptions about the person's disability. Labeled people frequently complain that staff members and parents ignore them for some reason. A few examples follow:

- John said to a staff member, "I want to speak to you." The staff member said it would have to wait until later. John repeated his request three more times, being very firm that he wanted to talk. The staff person also remained firm in ignoring him. Afterward, John explained, "She (staff member) doesn't understand me. If she did she would answer me ... she is too busy with many things."
- Will asked for a few dollars of his money that a staff member was holding for him. The staff member's response was that she would have to wait until tomorrow to talk. Will's response was, "She

always says that she is off-work now. She doesn't understand me. If she did, she would answer me."

C. Insensitivity to the Characteristics of their Disability: Another type of stigma-promoting barrier is to be insensitive or misinformed about a person's disability. Many people presume that people with cognitive limitations also have physical disabilities and vice versa. An example involved a vocational counselor and Hank, a consumer. A researcher was asking Hank to explain what he does at the workshop. Instead of allowing Hank to explain, the counselor, speaking in a very loud voice, said, "You put bolts in a bag, don't you? . . . You seal bags . . . You put bags in boxes . . . " It was apparent to both Hank and the researcher that the counselor was perceiving Hank as partially deaf and too stupid to speak for himself.

At times, human service workers have been observed talking in a very loud and demeaning tone to a consumer group when the consumers did not have hearing impairments. For example, Susan described such a situation: "She (staff person) treats everyone alike. She hollers at everyone. Some should be talked to loudly, but not others. If she would not yell but be gentle, she would get more cooperation."

5. Extreme Derogatory and Abusive Practices

Labeled people can also face extremely harsh encounters with stigma. These encounters include staring, ridicule and blatant rejection, and physical and sexual abuse. These incidents are most often perpetrated by strangers or others who do not know the labeled person well. However, staff and family members and other close associates have also been perpetrators.

A. Staring: Staring is one form of severe disregard for the feelings of labeled people. Numerous labeled people indicate keen awareness of others starring at them. As Louise explained, "Sometimes when I am waiting for a bus, people stare at me." She said that she knew they were staring even if she was not looking at them. She said, "It's like you feel it, and you turn around, and they are looking at you." Mary also said, "People stop and stare at me. It's okay with children. They don't know any better. But adults? It makes me angry. I feel like saying, 'Take a picture, it lasts longer!' "

B. Ridicule and Blatant Rejection: Incidents have been frequently identified in which labeled people are openly ridiculed. In one instance a stranger sat down next to Helen on a public bus and then got up and sat elsewhere after she caught a glimpse of Helen's appearance. The comments that followed between Helen and Dora indicated that this was not an isolated occurrence. Helen said, "Did you see that lady move?" Dora replied, "Yeah, that's why I gave her that look. People do that to me all the time."

In another instance, Louise was riding on the subway and two girls across the aisle were laughing. When they got off, they stopped laughing, confirming her suspicion that they were laughing at her.

Doc, who has difficulty walking, explained his experiences this way: "Every time I go out on the street, people laugh at me. I guess it's something that I do that people don't want me to do."

Other incidents involve staff members. One incident involved a staff member who amusingly imitated a consumer's mispronounced words with "She gets away with murther . . . ha ha." And George noticed that when he slouched in his chair, his staff member imitated him. And she also repeats what George says and hollers at him. His response was, "We have feelings like everyone else."

C. Physical and Sexual Abuse: At times, labeled people have reported that staff members, family members, and others have physically or sexually abused them, and these incidents have been corroborated by other reliable sources. One instance involved Sue who said that a staff person beat her because she lied. In another case, a labeled person who had attempted to sexually seduce a younger boy was forced into a brutal boxing match with a staff member who wanted to teach him a lesson. Other incidents were reported of staff members slapping or grabbing consumers for disobeying a rule or defying their authority.

6. Other Organizational and Programmatic Barriers

Stigma-promotion is an organizational or structural problem as well as an interpersonal one. Organizational and program barriers can be manifested by the mental retardation system and its programs in a variety of ways beyond some mentioned above.

A. Inappropriate Rules or Restrictions: Inappropriate program rules and restrictions are a manifestation of structurally-promoted stigma when they are based on misperceptions or disregard for the needs of labeled people. For example, restricting the freedom of all labeled adults on an outing may be the easiest way to insure the safety of the more vulnerable people in a large group. Yet, such a restriction should consider the capabilities of people in the group who can assume more independence. As another example, holding consumers accountable for breaking house rules is justified to maintain order at a residence. Yet, the staff response to breaking rules should help the consumers learn from their mistakes and assume increasing responsibility for their behavior.

In general, restrictions should be age-appropriate and individualized to each labeled person's needs to promote greater personal responsibility. Specific illustrations of inappropriate restrictions include:

- Ron was told that he could not attend a dance sponsored by a club for people labeled mentally retarded because the *staff* thought that the club members were too low functioning for him. Ron wanted to attend because he was attracted to some of the women there.
- Eating was not permitted on the second floor of a group home. Sol chose to eat part of his dessert in his room one night. His punishment was to be restricted to the house for a week. Sol felt that he should be permitted to eat food in his bedroom because he was willing to clean up any messes.
- Others have reported not being able to attend a community event because the staff members dictated that this was "chore night" or "shopping night" (Stevens, 1996).

Sometimes the language used to identify restrictions reveals its inappropriateness. An "allowance" was withheld from a 52-year-old woman. Another person was told "go to your room" when he got into an argument with another consumer. Phillip was placed on "probation" at his agency for hitting another consumer. His response was, "I don't need this (probation). It wasn't a big thing (hitting a consumer). I can go to City Hall and see people who are really on probation."

A blanket restriction imposed on an entire group can be a form of stigma-promotion when consideration is not given to individual differences. For example:

- All of the consumers of a mental retardation agency were prohibited from drinking alcoholic beverages at agency-sponsored events. Later, this restriction was amended to include only those without the written consent of a doctor. Some of the members who were more independent resented this restriction because they drank alcoholic beverages in other settings and felt foolish drinking soda at the agency's events while other adults drank alcohol.
- While on a vacation, George, who is a good swimmer, was told by

staff that he was not allowed to swim without supervision. He felt that he was being treated like a child, so he went swimming anyway.

- A number of consumers were prohibited from using the cafeteria at a workshop during lunch periods after one consumer changed the station on the radio. The others in this group had nothing to do with his actions.

- Another incident occurred during a vacation trip to another state; none of these consumers were allowed to go out on their own at night. The more experienced people resented being restricted because they were used to traveling freely at other times.

B. Segregated Programming: Many programs sponsored by the mental retardation system are segregated or exclude nondisabled people. This pattern occurs without considering alternative ways of doing things. Housing arrangements, work, and leisure and recreational needs of labeled people are still usually addressed through segregated service provisions.

Seldom, if ever, are programs designed as an integrated experience involving close associations between labeled and nonlabeled people. Also, generic agencies that provide similar services in the community are usually overlooked in favor of services of the System. Sometimes these generic services are not considered because a considerable amount of time may be required to train generic agency staff. Examples of socially integrated programs are highlighted in Chapter 8.

C. Overlooking More Valued Roles: The roles expected of consumers in this field are usually too narrowly defined. People with disabilities are expected to be dependent on the staff, cooperative and docile, and accepting of the status quo.

When they attempt to break out of these molds, they may be outgrowing a service or wishing to assume more of a leadership role. Expressions of anger, criticisms of staff members and programs, and requests to try something new may be their way of telling others that they wish to assume more responsibility for themselves. An example is a Maine consumer who shared a problem that she faced when speaking out: "I'm afraid to advocate for myself. When I am assertive, I am told I am pushy" (Jaskulski et al., 1990, p. 154).

More valued and normalized roles are often overlooked or discouraged for labeled people, partially because of misperceptions about their capabilities. New role possibilities for some people could include policy board member, spouse, parent, keynote speaker, lobbyist, homeowner, and supervisor to name a few. Unfortunately, these are unfamiliar roles in most mental retardation settings. Consumers express their views about this problem in the following examples:

- A plea for more opportunity to become independent came from a labeled person who said, "It is important for people with Down syndrome to become as independent as they can be. . . . People with Down syndrome should always try new things and be given a chance. Life is about trying new things and making new goals" (Jaskulski et al., 1990, p. 154).
- A Maine consumer pointed out: "Society does things to us and for us. I want to do things for myself. I want society to support my role as a functioning member" (Jaskulski et al., 1990, p. 197).

Examples of situations in which new more valued roles were overlooked are evident below:

- Eugene wanted to start a consumer committee to entertain severely disabled children in hospitals. The staff said that Eugene would need to have a staff person assigned to work with him in case he ran into problems. Eugene spent an entire year attempting to persuade the staff to help him, and he was still without staff support after the year had passed. Meanwhile, he held periodic meetings with other consumers to keep his dream alive—and with it a new role for himself.
- Another situation emerged in a consumer group. Roger, a consumer in this group, announced after meeting with the group for three months that he would no longer attend to get help because he did not need it. He said the he would continue coming to the group as an informal leader because he felt that he could help the other members by sharing his own experiences with them. Unfortunately, the group leaders did not actively support Roger's shifting role because his wishes were unusual and perhaps threatening as well.
- A final instance involved Ron, who was ill and wanted to be treated normally. In his words: "I was out of it. I just sat and wanted to watch TV. Then Mildred (a staff person) came in and yelled, 'What's wrong? What's wrong with your mind?'" Ron responded to the researcher: "I just wanted to be left alone, to be

able to lie in bed . . . when she (staff person) would come in (I would like) to turn over and tell her, 'It's just not my day'."

D. Insensitivity to Stigma Identifiers: Stigma identifiers can be unknowingly promoted by programs of the System. Arranging for a large group of labeled people to attend an outing together is an example.

Mixing a diverse group of consumers in one program is another example. Many program offerings, apparently attempting to be inclusive, offer the same services to everyone and seem blinded to each consumer's individuality and uniqueness.

People labeled with mental retardation function at different levels of independence and manifest varying degrees of stigmatization. Some people prefer to be in programs with others who are similar to them because they have more in common. Also, some may feel embarrassed if they are in a group with others having more obvious stigma identifiers.

An example of this problem occurred on an agency-sponsored trip to another state. Nancy and Roger chose to disassociate themselves from helping Mary, who needed to be pushed around in her wheelchair. These two travelers felt that they were on the trip to enjoy themselves and spending large amounts of their time caring for Mary was diverting them from their fun. Also, they seemed to want to disassociate themselves from the stigma identifiers inherent in Mary's physical condition. The staff members were persistent in their efforts to enlist Nancy and Roger to do what they felt was their moral responsibility — taking care of a peer, and they berated these consumers for their unwillingness to cooperate.

7. Other Violations of Civil and Human Rights

Most civil rights of people with disabilities in the United States are theoretically protected by federal and state laws. However, laws are violated whenever law enforcement is inadequate or not taken seriously. An Alaskan consumer shared an awareness of this limitation,

> There's a very important difference between acknowledging the right of an individual to full access to public services versus relegating such access to a social service agency and the 'helping the handicapped' frame of mind. (Jaskulski et al., 1990, p. 197).

Decisions of court case which emphasize the rights of labeled class members are an example of the need for greater enforcement of existing laws. Court decisions that have ordered states to abide by the least restrictive alternative, an environment free from harm and danger, or safe and appropriate use of medication, for example, are responses to flagrant violations of civil rights.

Discrimination against labeled people is evident in many areas, including employment, housing, health care, and access to buildings. As one labeled person exclaimed,

> Discrimination occurs in every facet of our lives. There is not an American with a disability who has not experienced some form of discrimination. Of course, this has serious consequences. It destroys healthy self-concepts and slowly erodes the human spirit. Discrimination does not belong in the lives of people with disabilities. (Jaskulski et al., 1990, p. 153)

Discrimination occurs in the hiring and promotion process, based on a person's disability. Also, housing has been denied to people numerous times solely based on misperceptions about their disabilities. Neighborhood opposition to small group homes is a prime example.

Health services are also denied people based on their disabilities. Dentists, for example, who will take labeled people as patients are difficult to find. A dramatic example of health care discrimination was a woman with Down syndrome who was rejected by two hospitals for heart and lung transplants (AAMR News & Notes, 1995). The reason given for the denial was that she did not have the intelligence to deal with the follow-up care and complications that could arise. This woman was a high school graduate, lived on her own, and had a state job busing tables at a cafeteria. Fortunately, she eventually received a heart-lung transplant, being the first known person with Down syndrome to receive one.

Labeled people with physical disabilities also have strong views about their right to access to buildings. One person stated, "One wish: that there was a more handicap accessible facility to use—whoever designed accessible bathrooms did not use a wheelchair" (Jaskulski et al., 1990, p. 155). Another person, Steve, complained that most of the time he needs help getting on and off the bus because the steps are so high. He commented, "I wish they would change those steps so either the old people or people like me won't have to ask for help all the time. . . . Any little thing helps, believe me" (Dorsey, 1985).

Numerous buildings, for example, are still not totally physically accessible even though the Americans with Disabilities Act was enacted in 1992. Unfortunately, to some, "wheelchair accessibility" may mean using a service elevator and going through the kitchen to get to your destination (Stevens, 1996).

Rights are violated in other areas as well. Jim had his rights violated when he unknowingly had a vasectomy at the same time that he was hospitalized for other surgery. He said that he did not know why his parents wanted him to have the vasectomy, but he ended up reluctantly going along with it because it seemed too late to turn back.

Rights are also overlooked in agency settings. Examples include excluding consumers from participating in the development of their individual habilitation plan, and forgetting to reevaluate an individual plan on a regular basis or at a critical time in the person's life.

Not having access to a guardian is another violation of consumers' rights. For example, one person complained, "Consumers assigned state guardianship haven't had any contact with their assigned representatives. Those being served are not even aware of the name of the person assigned to their case" (Jaskulski et al., 1990, p. 154).

References

AAMR News & Notes (1995). Woman with Down syndrome denied heart/lung transplant. Washington, D.C.: American Association on Mental Retardation, September/October, 1995.

Coleman, L. (1986). Stigma: An enigma demystified. In S. Ainlay, G. Becker, & L. Coleman (Eds.), *The dilemma of difference: A multidisciplinary view of stigma*, pp. 211–232. New York: Plenum.

Crocker, J., & Lutsky, N. (1986). Stigma and the dynamics of social cognition. In S. Ainlay, G. Becker, & L. Coleman (Eds.), *The dilemma of difference: A multidisciplinary view of stigma*, pp. 95–121. New York: Plenum.

Dudley, J. (1983). *Living with stigma: The plight of the people who we label mentally retarded*. Springfield, Il: Charles C Thomas.

Dorsey, S. (1985). Being handicapped. News Line Elwyn. Elwyn, PA: Elwyn Institutes, July, 1985.

Edgerton, R. (Ed.), (1984). *Lives in process: Mildly retarded adults in a large city*. Washington, DC: American Association on Mental Retardation.

Edwards, J. (1982). *We are people first: Our handicaps are secondary*. Portland: Ednick.

Goffman, E. (1963). *Stigma: Notes on the management of spoiled identity*. Englewood Cliffs, NJ: Prentice-Hall.

Jaskulski, T., Lakin, K., & Zierman, S. (1995). *The journey to inclusion: A resource guide for state policymakers*. Washington, D.C.: President's Committee on Mental Retardation, October, 1995.

Jaskulski, T., Metzler, C., & Zierman, S. (1990). *The 1990 reports: Forging a new era.*

Washington, D.C.: National Association of Developmental Disabilities Council, May, 1990.

Koegel, P., & Edgerton, R. (1982). Labeling and the perception of handicap among black mildly mentally retarded adults. *American Journal of Mental Deficiency,* 87(3), 266–276.

Lorber, M. (1974). Consulting the mentally retarded: An approach to the definition of mental retardation by experts. Unpublished doctoral dissertation, University of California at Los Angeles.

Research & Training Center on Independent Living (1990). *Guidelines for reporting and writing about people with disabilities,* Third Edition, 1990.

Stevens, K. (1996). Examples of stigma-promoting incidents were shared by Karen Stevens of the Integration Network of Western Massachusetts. Holyoke, MA.

Williams, P. & Shoultz, B. (1982). *We can speak for ourselves: Self-advocacy by mentally handicapped people.* Bloomington: Indiana University Press.

Wolfensberger, W. (1976). The origin and nature of our institutional models. In R. Kugel (Ed.). *Changing patterns in residential services for the mentally retarded,* Revised Edition Washington, D.C.: President's Committee on Mental Retardation.

Chapter 4

A SEPARATE WORLD

New Hampshire consumer: I just sit in my room, listen to the radio, have a cigarette . . . that doesn't cost anything. It's like a prison (Jaskulski, Metzler, & Zierman, 1990, p. 105).

A Georgia Consumer: We all need to work, play, and sleep. The people I know are sleeping and watching TV. It's not much to live for (Jaskulski et al., 1990, p. 105).

Susan: I plan to be like a normal girl someday.

From the perspective of many labeled people, there are two worlds—a "mentally retarded" world and a "normal" world. These two worlds typically exist side by side with very little social interaction occurring between them. People who are labeled with mental retardation are largely confined to a mentally retarded world.

Labeled people are not usually confined to a physical world like a mental institution. Rather the two worlds are set apart socially by the stigma that is associated with their disabilities.

Ironically, labeled people have almost complete access to the physical world of those without labels. To an extent, they are in close physical proximity to a fairly wide spectrum of nonlabeled people. People with disabilities spend more time than ever in the community, but not usually as an integral part of the community (Walker, 1995). Many of them frequent fast food restaurants, malls, movie theaters, hair dressers, and spectator sports events. However, these public settings require little if any interaction with others and are very unlikely to lead to continued social connections. Like other people frequenting these settings, labeled people remain socially anonymous.

Theoretically, there are numerous places where they could join others with similar interests in closer relationships. A few examples include dance classes, Bible study groups and church choirs, stamp clubs, informal work groups, softball teams, tennis clubs, neighborhood coffee klatches, YWCA exercise clubs, hiking clubs, and political party events. Such groups have great potential for friendships but are seldom explored. When these groups are considered, it is often done with much caution,

trepidation, and little optimism. And if labeled people attempt to participate in one of these groups, they seldom continue beyond one or two
attempts because they do not feel welcomed.

Phillip's circumstances are illustrative. Phillip had played table pool
at his recreation agency sponsored by the mental retardation system for
many years. He had become so skillful at playing the game that he
emerged as the best player at this agency, playing better than all of the
staff members and consumers. One day Phillip told everyone that he had
joined a table pool club in his neighborhood and would not be playing
pool so frequently at the agency. Months passed, and someone asked
him about his membership with the neighborhood pool club. He replied
that he had gone to the club only a couple of times and discontinued. He
changed his mind and decided to play table pool alone at home instead.
He offered no reason for his change of plans, but the explanation seemed
obvious—he felt unaccepted at the pool club.

What Is the Mentally Retarded World?

Perhaps separate worlds are not so bad, particularly if labeled people
meet their basic needs. Yet, a closer examination suggests that the
mentally retarded world is different from the outside world. Loneliness,
segregation, and limited opportunities for social connections are the
norm.

People living in the mentally retarded world spend most of their time
in places that are socially homogeneous, existing for labeled people only
(Walker, 1995). Most of their facilities are segregated from the mainstream,
including where they receive training, employment opportunities,
counseling, and leisure and recreation activities. Generally, they look to
their service providers within these mental retardation settings to fulfill
their needs. Many labeled people and their families would likely say that
they would have no other place to go to be with other people if the
System did not exist (Dudley, 1983).

How Do People Spend Their Time?

What do people do in their free time? One way to find out is to visit
one of their group homes or day programs. Many have discovered, when
making a visit, that the residents quickly approach you, desperate to
make contact, telling you their name, touching or hugging you (Amado,
1993b). Another frequently reported pattern of labeled people is to

engage in passive activities such as watching television, riding a bicycle up and down the street, or listening to the radio (Edgerton, 1989).

Labeled people are not disinterested in socializing with others. To the contrary, whenever there are opportunities to attend a social event sponsored by the mental retardation system, large numbers eagerly participate. Many would not miss such an event because of its importance.

A need for social connection is also evident in their persistent efforts to interact with each other at school and work. For example, I observed a night school program for people with disabilities that appeared to serve more as a gathering place for socializing with past and present friends and acquaintances than an academic program. Often the night school provided the only opportunity for these people to meet with one another.

The sheltered workshops also informally function as gathering places where friends can meet, pursue romances, and catch up on the news of other people in their common network of acquaintances (Dudley & Schatz, 1985a; Graffam & Turner, 1984). Observations of a researcher at one sheltered workshop illustrate this point (Dudley & Schatz, field notes, 1985b):

> Early on, I became aware of an active social network among the trainees. Almost all of them acknowledged that their close friends were at the workshop. They talked with friends at their table while they worked, gathered in groups during breaks, and danced alone and together during extended lunch periods when the music was turned on. Their discussions covered a wide range of topics. For example, one day there was talk about someone's new boy friend, a relationship breaking up, the whereabouts of old friends who left the workshop, a brother getting married, and the death of a relative. And their social contacts did not end when the work day was over. Even though these trainees were together for 35 hours each week, their evenings were often spent phoning each other to discuss the gossip of the day or social events coming up at the workshop.

What About Friends?

Loneliness is evident in the mentally retarded world. Loneliness is different from being alone, as most of these people are hardly alone. They are surrounded by human service workers and other consumers who are with them much of the time. While the extent of their loneliness may be difficult to measure, some have suggested that it can be reflected in the quality of their friendships and other social relationships (Chadsey-Rusch, DeStefano, Reilly, Gonzalez, & Collet-Klingenberg, 1992).

Several studies have investigated the friendships of labeled people, including how many friends they have. A national study inquired about the friendships of labeled people in small community living facilities (Hill, Lakin, Bruininks, Amado, Anderson, and Copher, 1989). Many of them had moved from larger to small community placements over the previous decade. Yet, the study found that large numbers were still without friends. One-third or more of the people surveyed in group homes and over 40 percent in foster homes had no friends at all.

Studies have also investigated how satisfied labeled people are with the number of friends that they have. In the national study reported above, Hill et al. (1989) found that the vast majority who had no friends were dissatisfied with their circumstances. Another recent study in North Carolina found that over three-quarters of the people residing in community and institutional facilities wished that they had more friends (Dudley, Ahlgrim-Delzell, & Conroy, 1995). Almost 20 percent of the North Carolina sample also reported having no friends. Other studies have had similar findings (e.g., Anderson, Lakin, Hill, & Chen, 1992).

Having friends does not necessarily mean spending much time with them. Anderson et al., (1992) found that approximately half of their sample of people over 60 years of age either had no friends or never saw the friends that they claimed to have. Only 25 percent of this sample who had friends saw them once a month or more often. The North Carolina study found that over three-fourths of their respondents complained that they were not able to spend enough time with their friends (Dudley et al., 1995).

Studies on friendship have also asked about the identities of their friends (e.g., Anderson et al., 1992; Dudley, 1983). In most instances, when they have friends, labeled people have other people with similar labels as close friends. They are roommates in group homes, members of the same special clubs, other employees at workshops, and associates from previous agencies. Sometimes these personal associations are long-standing ones that originated many years before in shared institutional experiences. Although deinstitutionalization may have moved them in divergent directions, these friends still attempt to maintain contact in a common workshop experience or through periodic phone calls.

Some labeled people have identified people without disabilities as friends too. Most often, the nondisabled friends are staff members who work with them. In most of these cases, however, it is unlikely that most of these staff members concur that they are close friends. These "friendship" are more often a fantasy of the labeled person or a casual association with the staff member that exists only at the agency setting. However, it is important to add that some of these friendships are real, reciprocal, and important (Lutfiyya, 1993).

Other people that are sometimes identified as friends are "outsiders," people without disabilities who do not work for the mental retardation system. Some of these friendships are genuine and very special to both people involved in the relationship (Amado, 1993a), but they are the exception. Other "outside friends" may not be seen very often, in some cases as infrequently as once or twice ever! In some cases, these are relationships that cannot be "bothered" too much for fear of losing them (Kaufman, 1984). In many cases, these outsiders may not even be real friends, but they are still important as symbols of what these people desperately want—friendships in the outside world.

Discontent is evident in the mentally retarded world. It is particularly evident among those who want to become more independent and lack success in developing friendships with outsiders (Dudley, 1983). Sometimes labeled people even complain that their residential program staff interfere with their efforts to have friends. Complaints include denying them privacy, screening the people who they can visit, and introducing program routines that interfere with their free time (O'Brien & O'Brien, 1995).

The Wall

A "wall" separates labeled people from the outside world of other people. One person with a disability compared this wall to the Berlin Wall with her comment:

> I also want you to know that integration is just getting started. It's like the Berlin where a big wall divided the city for years and years. On TV I saw people rush through the wall when they opened it up. No one got shot by the guards like they used to. But the wall is still there. The people on one side are still separated from the people on the other side. My Mom says its not just the wall that separates them now. It's their ideas, the way they live and think. For us who are handicapped, it's just about the same. (Jaskulski et al., 1990, p. 154)

Bio-Psychological Disability

This wall derives from the realities of their bio-psychological disabilities. Their disabilities, even though they are not formidable, stand in the way of their being accepted as "normal" people. Actually, their disabilities vary to a striking degree in nature and severity. Some people may have obtrusive physical deformities that are unappealing. A speech impediment, a noticeable limp, uncontrollable body movements, and childlike facial features are examples. In contrast, others may have no noticeable physical abnormalities and appear quite "normal" looking.

Virtually everyone who is labeled with mental retardation is likely to have some form of intellectual impairment. Some cannot readily converse in abstractions. Some seem only able to talk about themselves and their preoccupations. Some are slow in responding to all inquiries. Some seem unable to face simple challenges in their daily lives.

Yet, many labeled people present themselves as being quite astute intellectually, particularly as others get better acquainted with them. Some are able to carry a conversation on almost any subject, and some demonstrate unusual insights into their circumstances.

Besides physical and intellectual disabilities, many labeled people also reveal psychological problems or challenges. In most cases, these problems are a secondary derivative of their intellectual disabilities or their life experiences if they had been institutionalized. These psychological problems often become noticeable when they interact with others. For example, numerous labeled people lack assertive skills, and some can be extremely shy and withdrawn. Some interact with others by intruding in the other person's private space with unwanted physical contact or conversation. Countless numbers are misinformed in their attitudes toward sexuality or sexually behave in inappropriate ways. Relatively few have experienced a satisfactory sexual relationship, and some married couples even admit that they have never had sexual intercourse.

The Stigma of Disability

These bio-psychological disabilities, however, are not the primary reason for their separate existence. Labeled people are extremely diverse, and yet every one of them is set apart from the world of "normals." What they all have in common is the stigma associated with their disabilities.

Stigma derives from the stereotypes and myths that others project onto them because of their disabilities. Many in society have distorted perceptions of people who are labeled with mental retardation because they cannot see beyond their disabilities. This stigmatizing aspect of their identities carries such enormous significance for people that it overshadows other aspects of who they are.

The stereotypes and myths that society associates with mental retardation are certainly damaging. They include a long list of undesirable characteristics like being considered stupid, childlike, or unreliable. A more extensive list of stereotypes and myths are described in Chapter 3.

The characteristics of a person's disability that evoke negative reactions in others are not responsible for stigma-promotion, but they provide stimuli for it to happen. These most noticeable or obtrusive aspects of a person's disability serve as identifiers or symbols of stigma. Examples include slow responses to questions, age inappropriate behavior, inappropriate invasion of someone's space, inappropriate hugging, drooling, hand flapping, poor eye contact, volatile fits of anger, clumsiness, and speech impediments.

Because some stigma identifiers evoke such strong negative reactions in others, they can predict whether or not a person will succeed in community living. Actually, at times these stigma identifiers can be as important as the person's intellectual capacity in predicting success. For example, a person with an IQ score of 85 who also has cerebral palsy and an obtrusive speech drawl may have a greater chance of being rejected by others than a physically normal looking person with an IQ of 60. In some instances, these stigma identifiers may not even have anything to do with a person's intelligence. An obtrusive physical attribute like blindness or a cleft lip are examples.

In addition to these stigma identifiers that are personal characteristics of an individual, external cues can also be important identifiers of stigma. Consumers of the mental retardation system are likely to be carriers of some of these external stigma identifiers. Associating with other people having more severe stigmatic attributes can become a stigma identifier largely because it draws more attention to each person's stigmatic attributes. Affiliations with particular groups, programs, and organizations also can be identifiers of stigma. Being in the company of twenty people with a range of obtrusive disabilities, for example, is an obvious stigma identifier. Appearing at a social club sponsored by a mental retardation agency, living in a group home, or riding in an agency van are other examples.

Struggling with Stigma

Most labeled adults at the mild and moderate levels of mental retardation are likely to be keenly aware of the stigma that society associates with their disabilities. In some ways they may help to maintain the wall that divides them from others by tolerating its continuance. They perceive that they are stigma carriers, and every negative experience becomes a painful reminder of what they anticipate encountering on another excursion to the outside world. They may prefer to stay in their segregated world just to avoid being rejected. Conversely, many labeled people are determined to overcome the stigma in their lives. The strength of the self-advocacy is one powerful indication of that determination.

Labeled individuals behave like "normal" people. They are respectable, law-abiding citizens and express normal aspirations. A discussion occurring in a group session involving several labeled people illustrates their aspirations. The group facilitator asked the members to share their most important personal goals, and their responses were revealing. Almost all wanted to be employed and to earn a decent salary, some wished to have their own homes, and a few wanted to get married and to have their own children. Every member of the group mentioned at least one of these goals, and no one identified a socially unacceptable aspiration.

The values of labeled people may be no different than most United States citizens, with one exception. They probably spend more of their time obsessing on these aspirations. Maybe some are so intensely preoccupied with becoming self-sufficient and "normal" because the obstacles seem so overwhelming.

This obsessive desire to be normal is sometimes manifested as a need to cling to the normative attributes of others. The circumstances surrounding Roger's decision to get married illustrate this point. When he became engaged, the news of his marriage spread quickly throughout the agency because his fiancee was not labeled mentally retarded. The most important thing about her was her status as a "normal" person. One day Roger brought his fiancee to the agency to introduce her to others and in a sense to show her off. Ironically, she appeared to be the least physically attractive woman present at the agency that day. Yet, her lack of attractiveness was less important than the normal status that she represented.

In our society, being a person labeled with mental retardation is the antithesis of being "normal." There does not seem to be a continuum toward normality. Many labeled people, however, are not able to accept this dichotomy. They recognize that they are not fully "normal," and that they are different in some ways from others. But they perceive themselves to be more similar than different to others. And most do not identify themselves as "mentally retarded."

Nancy, who has struggled for a long time with the question of whether she is mentally retarded, finally decided, "I realized that I'm sort of what you call borderline. I'm in the middle—not here and not there." So it is with many labeled people—they are not mentally retarded, and they are not normal. Despite what others believe, they perceive themselves as being "somewhere in between."

Two worlds exist. The world of "normals" is not available to the vast majority of the people labeled with mental retardation. The next two chapters focus on the awareness that labeled people have of stigma and some of their strategies for coping with this social problem.

References

Amado, A. (Ed.) (1993a). *Friendships and community connections between people with and without developmental disabilities.* Baltimore: Paul H. Brookes.

Amado, A. (1993b). Preface. In A. Amado (Ed.). *Friendships and community connections between people with and without developmental disabilities* (pp. xi–xii). Baltimore: Paul H. Brookes.

Anderson, J., Lakin, K., Hill, B., & Chen, T. (1992). Social integration of older people with mental retardation in residential facilities. *American Journal on Mental Retardation,* 96(5), 488–501.

Chadsey-Rusch, J., DeStefano, L., O'Reilly, M., Gonzalez, P., & Collet-Klingenberg, L. (1992). Assessing the loneliness of workers with mental retardation. *Mental Retardation,* 30(2), 85–92.

Dudley, J. (1983). *Living with stigma: The plight of the people who we label mentally retarded.* Springfield, Il: Charles C Thomas.

Dudley, J., Ahlgrim-Delzell, L., & Conroy, J. (1995). Investigating the satisfaction of *Thomas S.* class members in year 1 & 2: Intermediate findings of two subgroups of class members with and without implemented plans, Monograph 5, Charlotte, NC: *Thomas S.* Longitudinal Research Study, August, 1995.

Dudley, J., & Schatz, M. (1985a). The missing link in evaluating sheltered workshops: The clients' input. *Mental Retardation,* 23(5), 235–240.

Dudley, J., & Schatz, M. (1985b). Unpublished field notes.

Edgerton, R.B. (1989). Retarded people of adult years. *Psychiatric Annals,* 19(4), 205–210.

Graffam, J., & Turner, J. (1984). Escape from boredom: The meaning of eventfulness in the lives of clients at a sheltered workshop. In R. Edgerton (Ed.), *Lives in process: Mildly retarded adults in a large city* (pp. 121–144). Washington, D.C.: American Association on Mental Retardation.

Hill, B., Lakin, K., Bruininks, R., Amado, A., Anderson, D., & Copher, J. (1989). Living in the community: A comparative study of foster homes and small group homes for people with mental retardation (Report No. 28). Minneapolis: University of Minnesota, Center for Residential and Community Services.

Jaskulski, T., Metzler, C., & Zierman, S. (1990). *The 1990 reports: Forging a new era.*

Washington, D.C.: National Association of Developmental Disabilities Council, May, 1990.

Kaufman, S. (1984). Friendships, coping systems, and community adjustments of mildly retarded adults. In R. Edgerton (Ed.), *Lives in process: Mildly retarded adults in a large city* (pp. 73–92). Washington, D.C.: American Association on Mental Retardation.

Lutfiyya, Z. (1993). When "staff" and "clients" become friends. In Amado, A. (Ed.). *Friendships and community connections between people with and without developmental disabilities.* Baltimore: Paul H. Brookes.

O'Brien, J. & O'Brien, C. (1993). Unlikely alliances: Friendships and people with developmental disabilities. In Amado, A. (Ed.). *Friendships and community connections between people with and without developmental disabilities.* Baltimore: Paul H. Brookes.

Walker, P. (1995). Community based is not community: The social geography of disability. In S. Taylor, R. Bogdan, & Z. Lutfiyya (Eds.), *The variety of community experiences: Qualitative studies of family and community life* (pp. 175–192). Baltimore: Paul H. Brookes.

Chapter 5

KEEN AWARENESS OF STIGMA

Jim: I won't say I am smart when I am not. I don't mind telling people I am slow.

TJ: I don't like being called retarded (Edwards, 1982, p. 22).

TJ: Many times you see what I am outside, but you don't see me inside. I am showing people what I can do outside and inside with my disability (as a leader in the self-advocacy movement). I am half deaf, and I have a label on me, mental retardation. I also have a number on me. It is 3328. That is a number that they give you in an institution. However, I don't look at myself as 3328 anymore. I look at myself as T. J. Monroe (Monroe, 1994, p. 10).

The public may think that people labeled with mental retardation have little awareness of their personal and social circumstances. More to the point, they may believe that labeled people have little understanding of their disabilities and the stigma in their lives.

Despite these public views, there is considerable evidence to the contrary. Many practitioners, researchers, family members, and others are coming to recognize the acute awareness that many labeled adults have. Evidence is mounting that labeled people are knowledgeable about their disabilities, have strong views about whether or not they are mentally retarded, and have keen sensitivity to the stigma in their lives (Dudley, 1983; Edgerton, 1984; Edwards, 1982; Lorber, 1974; Williams & Shoultz, 1982).

Knowledge of Their Disabilities

Labeled people have views about their disabilities and they describe them fairly accurately (Dudley, 1983; Zetlin & Turner, 1984). However, they have a strong tendency to avoid talking about their disabilities with most people. They are usually willing to discuss this private topic only after a safe and trusting relationship is established with someone.

Many labeled people are "qualifiers" or "vacillators" when talking about their disabilities (Turner, Kernan, & Gelphman, 1984; Zetlin & Turner, 1984). Rather than viewing themselves as "mentally retarded," they offer a less serious alternative for what is wrong with them. Many see themselves as slower than others, particularly in learning new things. For example, Karen explained, "I'm slow at times and it takes me three times longer than it would take someone else." Roger said, "I'm no different from the other guy. I can do what anyone can do. It just takes longer."

Others describe their disabilities using educational terms like reading, writing, counting, and budgeting. As Noreen explained, "I only have problems with reading, writing, and counting. I can do all of the housewife things . . . cook, sew, clean." Another similar explanation was, "I wasn't an "A" student. I was about a "C" student (Zetlin & Turner, 1984).

Labeled people having a medically-diagnosed condition such as cerebral palsy, are likely to view their disabilities in physiological terms. Mary explained, "I had encephalitis at 11 months and was damaged. Before that, I was a normal, healthy child. I have cerebral palsy which has affected my right arm and left leg, which I haven't control of. I can't walk without a cane or someone holding my hand." Another person explained that he had "a slight amount of brain damage" (Zetlin & Turner, 1984).

Others may attribute their circumstances to earlier behavioral problems. John explained, "My behavior was backward before. I got into fights a lot." He said that in his case, the reason that he was previously in a mental retardation facility was this behavioral problem, which his parents could not manage at home.

At times, individuals may reveal more introspection when they talk about their disabilities. They may go beyond labeling their disability as a learning or physical disability and describe its influence over their lives. Eugene talked about himself this way: "I may be slow in certain things. I might not be slow in certain things. It depends, you know. Possibly I can maybe do something better than they do. I don't know. I don't think I'm good at arithmetic. I guess I could do better." Paul explained, "I feel like I don't have everything all right but I have grown a lot over the years. I can walk good some days and not others. I can think well some days and not others. When I can't, its because I am upset, but usually I can carry a conversation with anyone."

Another person shared, "When you have like what you call mild retardation now . . . the wires in your brain sometimes get mixed up and that slows your thinking processes up and your learning gets set back.

You may be sick for six to eight years and meanwhile . . . if you were all goofed up like this, you're set back and you have a long haul in catching up and you can't move fast enough or achieve what you wanted to do . . . " (Andron, 1984).

Finally, some labeled people deny to others that anything is wrong with them (Dudley, 1983; Zetlin & Turner, 1984). These "deniers" either believe that they are like everyone else, or they may be attempting to conceal this vulnerable aspect of their identity. Scott said, "The only thing wrong with me is that I had a kidney disease when I was born." Ron explained, "The only thing I see wrong with myself now is my weight. Now you may have lots of other thoughts." Martin's explanation: "I say I'm a human being. I can do what they (people without disabilities) can do. I can work for all my own money. Every day I could go to the bus. One man sat there, talk to me. I talk back to him." "Deniers" may be reluctant to discuss their disabilities. When asked, they may say that they "don't know" or "don't want to go into all of that" and change the subject (Zetlin & Turner, 1984).

In many cases, labeled people view their disabilities not as a fixed condition but as one that is diminishing in importance. This view may include admission that their disability was once quite severe and debilitating, but now it seems milder and less significant. For example, Paul said, "I have learned how to get along as I got older." Ron shared, "I used to work seven to eight days in a row helping the cripples. One day I realized that I was not crippled or bent out of shape . . . I was a normal person and I didn't belong there." Another responded with brevity, "I used to be retarded, but I'm not any more (Zetlin & Turner, 1984).

Incorporated into many individuals' view of their disability is a sense of ambivalence about how debilitating it is. Some are not sure how much to admit to the difficulties that it imposes and how much to play down any difficulties as insignificant. The tendency seems to be to emphasize the insignificance of their disability. If the disability can be labeled as a localized, physical disability such as a speech defect or as a specific learning deficit, it is easier to accept and manage as part of who they are.

The Mental Retardation Label

For most labeled people, it may be comfortable to be viewed as a slow learner but not as "mentally retarded." Most labeled people do not even introduce the term, "mentally retarded." It is usually only raised for them in research inquiries or when they feel a need to express their disapproval of the label.

When labeled people have been asked in some studies whether or not they perceived themselves as "mentally retarded," their answers have been instructive (Dudley, 1983). Some are startled by the question, as if it is a taboo not to be mentioned. The majority are likely to deny that they are mentally retarded.

A closer examination of the responses of some who deny being mentally retarded reveals some of their feelings and views. Janet's response to the question was, "No . . . , I hate the word." Eugene, less angry, responded, "I don't think I'm retarded . . . I don't feel retarded." Karen explained, "No, I see myself as suffering from not starting at (a special school for people with disabilities) in kindergarten." She did not begin to attend this school until the age of sixteen.

A number of people reveal in their responses *why* they do not view themselves as mentally retarded. Examples are:

Phillip: No, . . . maybe a couple of years ago, but not since I have a job.

George: No, I don't. I was at X institution but not anymore . . . once in awhile I am mentally retarded.

Ron: No, I get up, go to work, work from eight to three, fix my own dinner, wash my dishes, don't answer to anyone.

Jennifer: I'm mildly retarded—why do they call me mentally retarded. That's for very low people.

Another: They can't read, can't hear well, can't see well. I can talk, I can read (Zetlin & Turner, 1984, p. 108).

Roger: When I think of the word "retarded," I think of people who are vegetables. They can't do anything for themselves.

The above examples reveal the definition of mental retardation to some. They portrayed it as a pervasive debilitating condition resulting in dependency and incompetence. For others, severe difficulties with speech and language in particular are a defining feature of mental retardation (Turner, Kernan, & Gelphman, 1984).

As stigmatic as the mental retardation label may be, some individuals, having previously internalized it as part of their identity, are "acceptors" and are willing to admit to having the mental retardation label, or at least expressing partial acceptance, for example:

One:	I'm mostly normal with slight retardation (Zetlin & Turner, 1984, p. 99).
Noreen:	No, I don't see myself as retarded . . . maybe half retarded.
Susan:	Not mentally retarded, mildly retarded.
Ann:	Maybe I am, maybe I can't learn things, but I think it just takes me longer.
Jill:	In some ways I'm retarded and in some ways I'm not. I'm afraid of people and don't like to get close . . . I'm afraid I will get treated bad as I did as a child.
Another:	I am a little handicapped, a little arthritis, a little mentally retarded . . . it means that I am a little slow (Zetlin & Turner, 1984, p. 99).

Most of the above examples reflect ambivalence or a lack of certainty about whether or not the label fits them. Yet, their views on this topic are usually expressed with intense feelings, suggesting that this question is crucial to the more general question of who they are.

Numerous reports from self-advocacy groups across the country support these findings pertaining to labels (e.g., Edwards, 1982; Jaskulski et al., 1990; People First of California, 1984; President's Committee on Mental Retardation, 1994; Williams & Shoultz, 1982). Self-advocates do not see themselves as "mentally retarded." Many find this label troubling and recommend its discontinuance.

Awareness of the Stigma Associated with Their Disabilities

The findings from several studies of labeled people also reveal that they have an awareness of the stigma associated with their disabilities and sometimes react with anxiety and anguish (Andron, 1984; Dudley, 1983; Turner, Kernan, & Gelphman, 1984; Lorber, 1974; Zetlin & Turner, 1984). All of these studies have used qualitative research methods and have required long-term relationships with the subjects in order to obtain data on this very sensitive aspect of their lives.

Labeled people's awareness is sometimes woven into their conversation on other topics. A few conversations are illustrative. While talking about her dating life, Karen was discussing the initial reactions that two new acquaintances might have toward each other when they first meet. She was planning to go out with a man who was blind, and she said, "He won't really be able to see me. I wonder if he knows about 'you know' (her mental retardation)?"

Jill, in referring to her dating life, said, "Men will not like me when they find out I am slow." Phillip revealed his awareness more subtly with, "I like women who work at my office but I wouldn't date them." When asked why, he said that they are either married or "higher educated" thus "don't want someone like me."

Often words that people use in conversing are themselves revelations of awareness of stigma. Some words like "slow," "borderline," and "more advanced" are used to describe themselves and their peers. Negative terms are sometimes selected to deride their peers who functioned at lower levels, for example, "baby," "low," "lower," "down," "vegetable," and "goofy" (Dudley, 1983; Turner, Kernan, & Gelphman, 1984). Or they could incorporate their awareness of stigma into an impulsive burst of anger, for example, yelling out "you raving idiot" and "that retarded bitch." Also, words can be used to distinguish other people without disabilities, such as calling them "normal" and "outsiders."

Other illustrations reveal the anguish and anxiety that can come from stigma. One person gives a vivid account of how it affected her: "It hurts more than a punch because you know you are (labeled) and everybody calls you it. But you don't want to say it. You know you are within . . . It's hurting you inside . . . Because they (other labeled people) feel they are and they know they are and they can't fight it . . . They're fighting themselves" (Andron, 1984).

Labeled people are also quite likely to feel the effects of stigma on their self-image, but it may be too difficult to share. Examples include feeling low self-esteem, lacking confidence in themselves, or developing a false or distorted sense of who they are.

Stratification Issues

A topic of special interest to some labeled people derives from the heterogeneity within their consumer groups. People with less obtrusive stigma attributes and more capacity for independence tend to stratify consumers using these criteria. Gibbons (1986) refers to this as a "downward comparison," or making comparisons between yourself and more stigmatized peers for self-aggrandizement. When an individual's self-esteem is continually being threatened, downward comparisons can serve as a boost; it can be reassuring that there is always someone else worse off than you (Wills, 1981). People who have less noticeable stigma identifiers are sometimes quick to point this out to "outsiders," that they are more like "normal" people than their more dependent peers with obtrusive attributes.

For example, Martin explained it this way: "I am able to hold a job. Others at my agency are not because they are lower level." Susan's explanation was: "We're our own boss and the others act like they're babies, but they're really not." Eugene confidentially told the researchers, "I almost didn't get into the agency initially because my IQ is a little higher than the others and I am smarter." In another example, Mary seemed to get to the heart of the issue, saying, "I like the people at the agency who are at my level. The others I don't have much to do with. They are too low. Not low low, but low. I have nothing against retardation. That is their handicap. But I don't need to be subjected to it."

Beyond identifying the differences between themselves and more dependent peers, some also express hostility, ridicule, and embarrassment. Roger and Phillip concurred that they would not date consumers at their agency. One told the other, "You can't talk to them. I have to get goofy to be with them." These two people relished recounting an experience at a recent agency-sponsored party. One joked to the other, "They (more dependent consumers) were grabbing all of the food as soon as it was served. One kept bumping into me while I was serving food. They acted like such babies!"

Paul shared his view with strong emotions, "Some clients are twenty-one and their bodies are like eight-year-olds. They aren't retarded though. Their parents are retarded. They hold them back and won't let them go out on their own." John said in a moment of unguarded reflection, "I wish I had a girl friend who was smarter. It bothers me when someone calls my girl friend 'retarded'." Finally, Martin recalled an agency-sponsored trip that he attended. He said, "They (more dependent consumers) were always fighting, yelling, or arguing. It was embarrassing. One of them called her boyfriend at five in the morning and woke up everyone in my room."

Labeled people who are more dependent and have more obtrusive attributes may not be considered desirable associates for people who are less stigmatized, particularly in public. Many people choose their associates based on the positive influence that they will have on their social acceptability. Karen illustrates this theme while recalling a recent restaurant experience with her roommate. "She (her roommate) kept bumping into the woman at the next table as she ate her salad." This infuriated

Karen because she felt that her roommate was oblivious to what she was doing. She added, "Just because she is retarded, she doesn't have to act it."

One might logically think that the labeled people who function fairly independently would be compassionate toward others functioning at lower levels. After all, the less stigmatized could feel fortunate that their disabilities are not so severe. Also, they surely share a personal abhorrence of stigma.

However, the central reality of stigma may overshadow a natural affinity for more stigmatized labeled people. People who function at lower levels of independence and have more obtrusive attributes may be too close in identity to embrace as close associates, particularly if "passing" is important (Goffman, 1963).

Nonetheless, rejecting more stigmatized people creates a new problem that also needs to be addressed. By derogating more stigmatized people, the less stigmatized are accepting and endorsing society's perception of stigma (Gibbons, 1986).

Stigma Associated with Agency Affiliation

Just as associations with more stigmatized people could be viewed as problematic, association with particular programs, living arrangements, and agencies create problems as well. Sometimes, mere affiliation with an agency creates a problem for some people. Some are aware of this, like Janet who was enrolled in a special night school program. After meeting a handsome male visitor at her school program, she commented on how attractive he was and then added, "He is going to think that I am stupid because I go to a dumb school." Karen, with similar awareness, was upset because her dates did not ask her out again once they discovered that she lived in a group home.

Programs that are not age-appropriate or challenging enough are derided by stigma-conscious individuals as well. The sheltered workshop programs are a notable example. Some of the comments of labeled people about their workshop experiences reveal their views.

Noreen:	I hated it.
Phillip:	I was lucky to leave that workshop after only a six-month stay. Some stay for two to three years.
Mary:	It (workshop) stinks. My job involves putting

screws in a bag, stuffing envelopes . . . It makes me feel like I'm retarded.

California Consumer: I work in a workshop and get paid very little money. I get $20 for two weeks of work. I don't think that's right, do you (Jaskulski et al., 1990. p. 71)?

Two labeled people who had never worked in a sheltered workshop had similar views. Martin said, "Thank goodness I never had to work in one of them." Eugene said, "I looked at one but would never go in there. I looked at X workshop, I felt higher than that. I'm stuck in the middle . . . I'd rather stay home than go to a workshop."

Two others felt so strongly about not working in a sheltered workshop that they advised their peers against it. Paul said to another, "Get wise, leave the workshop and get a real job." Phillip, in speaking to a group of consumers in a day program about his job with city government, concluded with the advice, "Take any job to get out of the workshop."

Some of the complaints about sheltered workshops explain why these people are so adamant in their views. Ron explained, "Usually they don't have anything for us to do, and I still have to go every day. It makes me angry that I have to go to work and then there is nothing to do." Hank reflected on a previous workshop experience, saying, "I could do better. Putting a sponge in a paper bag . . . I could do more than that. Others might need it though."

Some complain because they make so little money and do not have opportunities to advance. Roger, a former trainee of a sheltered workshop, became angry while recalling his experience. "I was kept down. When I tried to advance to a higher level of work, I was changed to another job. The staff there wouldn't let me talk for myself. I was working for pennies."

As these illustrations point out, the type of work, the inadequate advancement opportunities, and the meager salaries partly explain why the workshops are despised. Some may also have a subconscious fear of never leaving a workshop and holding a regular job. It is also suspected that the heterogeneity in the consumer population in a workshop is a problem for those who are more stigma conscious.

Variations in Stigma Awareness and Diversity Issues

Stigma awareness may vary among different groups. This may be particularly true with regard to preoccupation with stratification issues. Agencies having a consumer group with considerable heterogeneity in their disabilities as opposed to homogeneity may be more likely to have some who are concerned about stratification issues because of this reality. This was evident in one study when comparisons were made between agencies with heterogeneous and homogeneous consumer populations (Dudley, 1983). A community's degree of acceptance of labeled people may also influence whether or not there is preoccupation with these issues; more community acceptance will probably diminish this type of concern (Dudley, 1983; Henshel, 1972).

In conclusion, it seems that labeled people are much more aware of their personal and social circumstances than many people think. Sometimes their awareness is keen, particularly about the stigma associated with their disabilities.

References

Andron, L. (1984). The experts discuss retardation: Labeled as retarded, they now speak for themselves. Unpublished paper, Neuropsychiatric Institute, UCLA, Los Angeles, CA.

Dudley, J. (1983). *Living with stigma: The plight of the people who we label mentally retarded.* Springfield, Il: Charles C Thomas.

Edgerton, R. (Ed.), (1984). *Lives in process: Mildly retarded adults in a large city.* Washington, D.C.: American Association on Mental Retardation.

Edwards, J. (1982). *We are people first: Our handicaps are secondary.* Portland: Ednick.

Gibbons, F. (1986). Stigma and interpersonal relations. In S. Ainlay, G. Becker, & L. Coleman (Eds.), *The dilemma of difference: A multidisciplinary view of stigma*, pp. 123–144. New York: Plenum.

Goffman, E. (1963). *Stigma: Notes on the management of spoiled identity.* Englewood Cliffs, NJ: Prentice-Hall.

Henshel, A. (1972). *The forgotten ones: A sociological study of Anglo and Chicano retardates.* Austin: University of Texas Press.

Jaskulski, T., Metzler, C., & Zierman, S. (1990). *The 1990 reports: Forging a new era.* Washington, D.C.: National Association of Developmental Disabilities Council, May, 1990.

Lorber, M. (1974). Consulting the mentally retarded: An approach to the definition of mental retardation by experts. Unpublished doctoral dissertation, University of California at Los Angeles.

Monroe, T. (1994). Self-advocate's perspective. In President's Committee on Mental

Retardation, *The national reform agenda and people with mental retardation: Putting people first*, pp. 9–10. Washington, D.C.: U.S. Department of Health and Human Services, April, 1994.

People First of California (1984). *Surviving in the system: Mental retardation and the retarding environment*, Sacramento: California State Council on Developmental Disabilities.

President's Committee on Mental Retardation (1994). *The national reform agenda and people with mental retardation: Putting people first*, pp. 9–12. Washington, D.C.: U.S. Department of Health and Human Services, April, 1994.

Turner, J., Kernan, K., & Gelphman, S. (1984). Speech etiquette in a sheltered workshop. In R. Edgerton (Ed.), *Lives in process: Mildly retarded adults in a large city* (pp. 43–71). Washington, D.C.: American Association on Mental Retardation.

Williams, P., & Shoultz, B. (1982). *We can speak for ourselves: Self-advocacy by mentally handicapped people*. Bloomington: Indiana University press.

Wills, T. (1981). Downward comparison principles in social psychology. *Psychological Bulletin*, 90, 245–271.

Zetlin, A., & Turner, J. (1984). Self-perspectives on being handicapped: Stigma and adjustment. In R. Edgerton (Ed.), *Lives in process: Mildly retarded adults in a large city*, (pp. 93–120). Washington, D.C.: American Association on Mental Retardation.

Chapter 6

COPING WITH STIGMA

Eugene: I'm different than I was when I was new (at the agency) fifteen years ago. I'm more outspoken now, and probably most people don't like it.

Roger: Before I worked at refinishing furniture at Goodwill Industries. I'd tell others I refinish furniture at Goodman Industries or something else. I had to lie . . . which isn't good . . .

Even though recognition may be given to the adverse and demeaning effects of stigma, not enough consideration is given to how labeled people actually cope with it. This chapter describes some of the ways that they can cope and adapt. Truly, these coping qualities are some of the special strengths of labeled people.

Stereotypes abound about whether or not labeled people can cope with stigma. They are often viewed as helpless victims of their social circumstances. Possibly they are thought to be incapable of confronting another person's prejudice or managing themselves when faced with ridicule. Or perhaps a prevalent view is that the burden of defending themselves is too much to expect on top of the heavy burden that they already carry.

When the heterogeneity of this population is considered, including the wide range of disabilities and life experiences, it seems obvious that there is also considerable variation in how people manage the stigma in their lives. An important question to explore is "How do many of them do it?"

Theoretical Considerations on Coping

According to Goffman (1963), stigmatized people can choose between being "discredited" or "discreditable." If they choose to be discredited, they assume that their differences are known by "normals" with whom they are in contact, and they concentrate their energies on *managing the tension.* People with a mental retardation label are often faced with such

65

tension, resulting from problems like ridicule, staring, or a demeaning comment.

In the discreditable situation, stigmatized people assume that their differentness is neither known about by those present nor immediately perceivable by them. In this instance, they can concentrate on *managing information about their stigmatic attributes* so that they will not be exposed and rejected. Goffman calls this the option of "passing as a normal." He suggests that this may be a feasible option for some stigmatized people. Many people with a mental retardation label have been known to pass by concealing their stigma identifiers and pretending that their disability did not exist. This phenomenon will be explored later.

Lemert (1972), another sociologist, develops a different perspective. He argues that stigma-promoting processes usually cannot be successfully contained. Instead, these problems can be manipulated to the advantage of the stigmatized. He calls this option seeking the *positive side of a negative identity,* which can take many forms.

People with a mental retardation label have been known to manipulate the "positive side of their identity." They have many opportunities to seek out the "positives" of being stigmatized. For example, they have opportunities to make new friends if they become consumers of an agency serving a group of stigmatized people. They can receive many special services and the personal attention of a group of caregivers. They can also use their stigmatic status to elicit pity when they are in public.

In brief, Lemert would view stigma as a force that can be exploited by maintaining it. Goffman gives more attention to the various ways to overcome or reduce its deleterious effects. These two theorists take different views of the same general phenomenon and raise significant questions: Can stigma be significantly mitigated? Can some people who are labeled with mental retardation pass as "normal" to lessen the effects of stigma? Or is it more realistic to view the stigmatic attributes of labeled people as unalterable, leaving them with no choice but to adapt?

An additional set of questions, moral in nature, also need to be asked: Even if people with a mental retardation label are capable of passing as "normal," should this be encouraged? Will passing create more problems for them because they know that they are not "normal?" Lemert suggests that as long as people keep trying to be what they know they are not, their problems will continue. All of these questions raise dilemmas for labeled people that they will need help in considering.

Five Strategies of Coping

Five general types of responses to stigma have been identified. The first type portrays labeled people in a beginning phase of learning how to cope with stigma, while the other types could be viewed as strategies taken as individuals become more proficient in their efforts.

This presentation is not an exhaustive coverage of strategies of coping with stigma, but rather a beginning exploration. All but the first pattern are supported by the theoretical conceptualizations of Goffman or Lemert.

1. Beginning Attempts to Cope with Stigma

Encounters with stigma often cause anguish for labeled people. A belittling remark, a cold stare, or willful disregard of a person's viewpoint hurts some individuals in unimaginable ways. The pain derives not only from each stigma-promoting incident but also from the cumulative effect of countless previous incidents. The latest incident is just another reminder of their inferior status.

When labeled people are asked how they feel about their encounters with stigma, the most frequent response may be to avoid talking about it or to minimize its importance. The bus scene mentioned in Chapter 3 in which a passenger sat next to Helen, noticed her, and then moved to sit somewhere else, brought pain to Helen. The way that she chose to cope with it was to get off the bus and walk the rest of the way home alone.

Many individuals, when asked how they feel about such encounters, have said something like, "I don't want to think about it," "I don't let it upset me," or "I don't want to talk about it." Yet it is evident, in most of these cases, that the experiences can be painful . . . and difficult to share.

Paul revealed both the intensity of his feelings and his reluctance to respond. He said that a stigma-promoting incident with a staff person upset him so much that he could not work well at his job for an entire week. Nevertheless, he chose not to tell the staff member how he felt.

Helen, when asked how she felt about being called mentally retarded, expressed her pain by saying, "I feel invisible . . . half down. I feel like nothing. I have been called dumb and crazy and on these occasions I sometimes get angry and tell people to get away . . . or I just walk away."

Overall, people who are beginning to learn how to cope with stigma usually have no conscious strategy. In this situation, people seem to realize and feel the discomfort of stigma, but they have little capacity to manage it or to know what to do about it. Their reactions to stigma are usually not premeditated; most often they represent a set of haphazard responses to rid themselves of the pain.

I believe that this tendency to be unprepared and defenseless in the face of stigma is associated with how well labeled people understand the origins of their stigma problems. People with this tendency are not sure whether to blame themselves or the perpetrator. Doc, who has cerebral palsy that restricts his mobility, revealed his confusion when he said, "Every time I go out on the street, people laugh at me. I guess it's something that I do that people don't want me to do. I don't walk straight. I can't walk straight." He added, "A strange feeling comes over me when I walk. You think you're no good, that you will step on people's toes."

The confusion about who is responsible for stigma problems derives from the confusion that labeled people have about their identities. The question of whether or not they perceive themselves as "mentally retarded" can be relevant to this confusion. Jill illustrates this when she said, "In some ways I'm retarded and in some ways I'm not. I'm afraid of people and don't like to get close. I'm afraid I will get treated as I did as a child." Jill was mistreated at an earlier time in her life when she was considered mentally retarded. As an adult she is still influenced by her childhood experiences, but she is also beginning to question her earlier identity.

A shifting identity characterizes many labeled people as they get older. As children they may have passively accepted the mental retardation label and their status as a mentally retarded child. But now that they are adults who live in the community and assume increasing responsibility for themselves, their self-perceptions are changing. To varying degrees they feel ambivalent about their disability status and many have an increasing conviction that they are more normal than disabled.

However, this change in their identity does not seem to be a consistent move forward; their feelings and perceptions tend to vacillate between these two conflicting identities—being "mentally retarded" and "normal." Many factors thwart their movement toward a more normal identity, including their internal tapes from the past; the confusions that their parents, staff members, and others convey about their identities; and their continued encounters with stigma promotion in all aspects of their lives.

This state of ambivalence about their identities is likely a developmental one. As labeled people become increasingly responsible for themselves psychologically, economically, and socially, they are able to gain greater conviction about who they are. Furthermore, as they are able to reassess their identities and the nature of their disabilities, they gain new perspective on the stigma in their lives.

Four additional strategies of coping with stigma are important to consider. Two of these strategies, seeking the "positive aspects" of being labeled and confronting stigma, are direct and open encounters with stigma. The other two strategies, passing and covering, involve managing and concealing aspects of their identities as a means of coping.

2. Seeking the "Positive Aspects" of Stigma

One tendency that labeled people have is to allow stigma promotion to happen and to even actively invite it if benefits are available. Lemert (1972) identifies this tendency as promoting "the positive side of a negative identity." Lemert believes that the stigma associated with a deviant identity is not likely to be contained, particularly for those who deviate significantly from society's norms. The alternative is to enlist efforts that will make the most of a deviant situation. Unfortunately, some types of stigma promotion become solutions for some individuals, particularly when secondary benefits are available.

One stereotyped image of labeled people encourages the tendency to seek the "positives." This image characterizes these people as objects of pity (Wolfensberger, 1976). Labeled people are pitied because they are perceived as victims of a condition over which they had no responsibility. Thus, there is interest in bringing happiness to them but without any serious attempt to develop their competencies and independence.

This image takes visual form when a labeled person ventures out into the community. The stigma identifiers of an individual may elicit sympathy from some people in public places. Strangers may wish to do something, however small, to "help," setting in motion an exchange that is likely to promote the positive side of a negative identity.

An incident involving Ann illustrates this. Ann, a petite woman who can project a vulnerable image, manipulated her circumstances one evening while waiting in the rain with her peers for a bus. She and her two friends were beginning to get soaked because they had forgotten their umbrellas. A woman appeared, and before long, Ann was invited to join the woman under her umbrella. The woman protectively placed her arm around Ann and upon boarding the bus invited Ann to sit by her.

Meanwhile, Ann's two friends sat several seats behind them and mused about her shrewdness.

Similarly, behaving as a docile, dependent consumer of an agency may bring positive benefits. A subtle collusion can easily develop between caregivers and consumers which keeps consumers compliant, incompetent, and "retarded" (Levine & Langness, 1986). The caregiver gains a smooth running agency operation and the consumer can expect a service with a predictable and undemanding environment. Ron shared his understanding of what happens when he behaves in this way at his agency. He said that by being "nice" he is called "honey bunch," "sweetie pie," and "handsome" by the staff. He feels ambivalent about his circumstances, however, as he added: "Be nice and you'll get a lollipop or ice cream . . . That's when I was a child . . . Now I am a man."

The mental retardation system in general has a tendency to promote the "positives" of being a person with a disability. Consumer status in this system provides people with many services and opportunities that would otherwise be denied them. One opportunity in particular is a social context for consumers to meet and develop relationships with each other. Friendships, romantic relationships, and other explorations of common interest all become possible when a person becomes a consumer of the System. Without this System, virtually none of these associations would develop.

John, who worked at a sheltered workshop, had developed a long-term romantic relationship with a young woman who also worked there. In the past, John was able to visit his woman friend at her family's home, but her father decided to stop these visits. This action left John with only one place to see her—at the workshop. He took advantage of every opportunity available to him to be with his girl friend, including coffee breaks, lunch, and immediately before and after workshop hours. He privately admitted that the sole reason he wanted to be a consumer of the workshop was to be with her, and he was determined not to take an outside job because it would mean abandoning her. John's circumstances suggests that the mental retardation system has a valuable contribution to make in offering opportunities for friendship, but such opportunities could thwart other agency goals like obtaining outside employment and greater self-sufficiency.

Another special benefit of the mental retardation system is the access that consumers have to a group of attractive, sensitive, and caring people—the staff members. These employees can easily foster special attachments with individual consumers, whether consciously motivated or not. In most cases, these attachments are not readily available to labeled people outside the System.

When asked to identify their closest friends, many labeled people mention favorite current or former staff members. In most cases, the staff members would probably not concur that the relationship was a genuine friendship, at least not outside the agency. But the fact that these relationships exist is very important to many consumers.

A physically attractive female staff member with an equally vibrant personality provides an illustration of this point. She was the program director of an agency and a very popular staff member as well. It was not uncommon for her to have a trail of consumers following her wherever she went, and many of the male consumers shared fantasies of being her lover, husband, or special friend outside the agency. Undoubtedly these consumers would not have had this association if she were not a staff member.

Agencies can also be perceived as reinforcing the positive side of being labeled because the recipients of their programs must be labeled to be eligible. Group homes and supervised apartments are examples. They provide well-furnished, government-subsidized living units, and a primary eligibility requirement is that the occupant be labeled with mental retardation.

Karen expressed understanding of this secondary gain when an apartment became available to her. She had lived her entire life with her mother, and at the age of 28 she wanted more freedom to date and assert her independence. As she explained it, "I would still be living at home if it hadn't been for being mentally retarded."

Another example are the special vacation clubs that offer trips for labeled people to travel to far away places like Israel, England, and Hawaii. Previous to joining these clubs, some people may not have traveled outside their town or county without being accompanied by their parents. Now some of them are traveling abroad with supervisory staff, staying at first-class hotels, eating at fine restaurants, and touring well known, popular sights. All this is possible because they qualify as labeled people.

Promoting the positive side of being labeled is not necessarily bad. The mental retardation system clearly meets many basic needs of its consumers, and most of these needs would probably go unmet if the

System did not exist. In many ways the System helps consumers develop their competencies and experience a more normalized life.

Nevertheless, in some instances the System's services have a harmful effect (Schwartz, 1992). More attention could be given to understanding the "secondary benefits" of the mental retardation system that foster stigma and discourage consumers from becoming more competent and self-sufficient. Some agencies may also need to uncover some of the ways that they discourage their consumers from terminating from services when the services are no longer needed.

3. Confronting Stigma

Another option available to labeled people is to directly confront the stigma that they encounter. At one time, the advocacy role was thought to be beyond the capabilities of these people. In recent years, however, that view has been forcefully challenged. The growing strength of the self-advocacy movement provides ample evidence of the capacity of many individuals to be advocates.

Yet, most labeled people probably still do not believe that they can be self-advocates. Their previous socialization has convinced them that their views must be represented by other people; their role is to remain acquiescent, cooperative, and grateful for the opportunities that they already have. Such individuals need help in realizing both their potential and developing capacity to be their own agents of change.

In my experiences, most labeled people seem reluctant to speak out when their needs are disregarded or minimized. They feel vulnerable in their roles as consumers. People in authority, particularly their parents and staff members who supervised aspects of their lives, have considerable control and influence over what happens to them. Labeled people are well aware of these external sources of control.

Nonetheless, some labeled people are critical of their circumstances and at times seem ready to take courageous steps to confront the barriers to their development. As Eugene said, "I'm different than I was when I was new (at the agency) fifteen years ago. I'm more outspoken now, and probably most people don't like it."

The actions of a group of consumers reveals an example of confronting stigma (Dudley, 1983). They actively confronted the executive director of their agency for inappropriately using the mental retardation label when referring to the consumers of the agency in a fund-raising drive.

They did not perceive the label to be an accurate descriptor, and they were demanding its discontinuance. Several discussions with the director led to an impasse, and then these consumers asked to meet with the agency's board of directors to discuss this matter further. A lively emotional exchange ensued at the board meeting between consumers and board members. Both sides aired their views and listened to the other side in a new fresh way. While the board decided to take no action on changing the labels that they used, changes were gradually instituted in an informal way by the director over time. This consumer effort was both successful and empowering for all who were involved.

Other examples of confronting stigma are worth noting. Karen wrote a letter to the director of the hospital where she was employed to complain about the way that some staff members interacted with other staff members, like her, who had disabilities. In her letter, she stated that she wondered how they would be able to deal with all the different types of people whom they serve if they did not develop more sensitivity for those with whom they work. She was still waiting for a reply to her letter eight months after she had sent it.

Change often is sought when someone feels mistreated. Anger about the mistreatment serves as the underlying catalyst for seeking redress. While many people with disabilities may not be comfortable expressing anger, some do express it.

Sometimes their anger is expressed as a defiant act such as laughing at or deliberately ignoring an order issued by a staff person. Occasionally, anger is expressed openly in the form of rage. Some labeled people express their anger openly to others, once they realized that it will not lead to negative consequences such as a reprimand or suspension from a program.

Ron talked angrily about "the big shots" when describing how he was denied a part in the decision to transfer him to another residence. Phillip aired his feelings with a researcher after knowing him for about a year. He was referring to the staff of his agency when he blurted out, "When are you guys going to wise up? You got to know what you are doing. You wouldn't treat yourselves that way." Patricia also dramatically expressed her anger with, "We're not asking for your blood—we're just asking to be treated as you'd want to be treated, if you were in our position (Killius, 1982, p. 82)."

Another labeled person expressed his anger in a group session with others; he was sharing how he might respond to someone calling him "mentally retarded," " . . . You either laugh it off or ignore it. Or the third one, you get mad and you say "Who the hell do you think you are? If you think I'm stupid, why don't you look at yourself in the mirror after you have said it and take a look at yourself for saying that . . . that makes you even more stupid" (Andron, 1984).

One individual reminds us that educating others about stigma can be done using humor. He illustrated, " . . . I took the subway. I was standing up, and there were two women there, one sitting down. The one who was standing said, 'Oh, give the poor kid your seat. He's sick.' I said, 'I was okay when I left the house this morning. I didn't have a fever' " (Carabello, 1982, p. 78).

These expressions of anger may not be frequent occurrences for many people, but when they occur they are significant and should be given special attention and encouragement. Expressing anger about one's circumstances is often an important step in taking more control over one's life.

4. Passing

According to Goffman (1963), many stigmatized people discover at some time in their lives that they can "pass" as someone with a less stigmatic identity or even as a "normal" person. While passing may not be an option for labeled people who have obtrusive stigmatic attributes that are unalterable, it is a potential option for many others.

The inclination to develop proficiency in passing may be strong because of the advantages that can accrue from being perceived as "normal" or less stigmatic (Goffman, 1963, p. 79). Passing may first be experienced unwittingly, without the person realizing that it is occurring. The next stage may involve more conscious awareness about passing as it is occurring. From there, a person may pass for fun or nonroutine activities. Finally, a person may develop a capability to pass in more important places like work, in their neighborhood, and while using public services.

Passing is not a topic that is openly discussed; nor is it easy to observe. This should not be surprising because the nature of passing is to conceal an unpleasant aspect of one's identity. Some of the manifestations of passing that have been observed involve insignificant activities. Some individuals purchase books or magazines and display them among their belongings so that outsiders can see them even though they cannot read (Levine & Langness, 1986). Some will claim that they forgot their glasses when called upon to read, or wear a broken watch in case they are asked the time. Some even purchase a car that does not run to present a highly positive symbol to others.

Sol was observed purchasing a newspaper and carrying it home on the bus even though he cannot read. Apparently he was attempting to portray himself as a typical bus passenger reading a newspaper like everyone else. Eugene usually chose not to count his change when making a purchase at a store because the excessive time that he would need would give him away. He admitted to doing this when he said, "I know I have to train myself to get the change. I can figure it out, but it takes me a couple of seconds longer. I know how to count, but to make sure I get the right change (is difficult) . . . I should check it more closely than I do sometimes. I just take the change and that's it . . . I guess whatever a person wants to do they can do."

Sometimes passing involves concealing associations with other people who have more stigmatic attributes. An interesting example of this took place on an agency-sponsored trip to a baseball game. Two consumers who did not have noticeable stigma identifiers chose to disassociate themselves from the other consumers. Both did this by walking a short distance behind them on the way into the ball park and by leaving alone just before the game ended.

In other instances, passing has been observed to be more vital to the individual's basic needs. Janet, being acutely aware that the group home where she lived could be a giveaway of her status, decided to tell her male dates that her home was a place where people pay board. Dede knew that men would most likely not initially accept her disability, so she tried to conceal it until after a man began to like her. She reasoned that her delayed self-disclosure would increase her chances that he would continue to like her.

Five people who had previously been institutionalized attempted to hide or minimize their status when asked by a researcher why they had been there. Their explanations reflected a problem much less severe than mental retardation.

Sol: I was there to help out the others. That's what the staff told me.

John: My behavior was backward.

Scott: I was there for two reasons. My mother didn't have the money to take care of me and I got caught stealing with my cousin.

Doc: The school I went to was torn down and my mother couldn't
            take care of me anymore because she had four jobs, so I went
            to (the institution).
George: I was fighting all the time. I first went to X Hospital because
            I had seizures and had to take medication. Then I went to
            (the institution).

These five people were denying that they had a mental retardation
label and were offering an alternative reason for their institutionalization,
which may have also been true. As was described in Chapter 5, many
individuals deny being mentally retarded, and one of the motives is to
pass as someone with a less stigmatic identity.

Roger revealed the anxiety that can be involved in attempting to pass
when he said, "At a place with other people, you have to . . . they go
around and each says something. One says he is in college, taking
psychology. Another is a speech therapist. The next one says she is a
teacher, and when it gets to me, I say I graduated from high school and
work for the government as a clerk. It (the job) doesn't knock you
down . . . builds you up. A guy that sweeps floors, it doesn't do anything
for you. Here I have a skill, work in an office. Before I worked at
refinishing furniture at Goodwill Industries. I'd tell others I refinish
furniture at "Goodman" Industries or something else. I had to lie . . . which
isn't good, but now I don't have to."

Goffman (1963) describes the final phase of passing as one in which
passing occurs in all aspects of one's life, with the secret being known
only to the "passer" and possibly to a few additional people who assist in
the concealment. In this phase, a person who has been labeled with
mental retardation and has lived in the mentally retarded world would
be prepared to leave it to live in the normal world. This option is
explored further in Chapter 12.

5. Covering

The final strategy of coping with stigma, "covering," refers to instances
when people are willing to admit that they possess a stigmatic attribute
but attempt to keep the stigma from looming large (Goffman, 1963).
The stigmatized person's objective is to divert attention away from the
stigmatic attribute so that more normal interaction can occur. As one
consumer explained, "(To get people to stop calling you names) you

have to take away what you are doing wrong if it is something you can take away (Andron, 1984).

Covering can be employed in social situations in which a person's stigmatic identity is either known or not. It is different from passing in that the person is willing to admit to possessing a stigmatic attribute. Admittance is a necessity in settings where one's identity is already known or when a stigmatic attribute is immediately apparent. Covering could also be viewed as a special form of passing in situations where the person's identity is not known. In other words, just because one is willing to admit to the possession of a stigmatic attribute does not necessarily mean openly volunteering this information.

Covering is an option that is widely supported within the mental retardation system. Central to normalization philosophy is the view that people with disabilities should appear and behave as culturally normative as possible in order to be accepted in the community (Wolfensberger, 1972). Staff members who follow normalization principles often place emphasis on helping their consumers dress appropriately, follow good grooming practices, develop conversation skills, and respect the established norms of a neighborhood. Normalization philosophy also promotes "normalized" programs and services in the community.

Covering can be observed in numerous social situations. It is revealed in the fashionable clothing and hair styles of many labeled people. It is often manifested in program objectives. Examples include teaching skills in banking, shopping, using make-up, traveling on public transportation, dating, and other routine aspects of living. One agency teaches its consumers the latest dance steps in case they decide to venture out to a dance club or bar.

Most of the instances of covering involve the active support of staff members and parents; their intentions are to enhance the attractiveness and repertoire of skills of the people involved. Labeled people seem to freely partake in these activities, and generally seem in favor of their objectives. However, they rarely describe such activities as attempts to "cover" or minimize their obtrusive attributes. Like the act of passing, covering is too closely linked to their sometimes fragile identities and is not an appropriate topic for discussion. The act of covering should probably have its own "cover"—being described as a part of the maturation into adulthood or an effort to stay up with the times, rather than as a means of minimizing stigma.

In summary, the variety of ways in which many labeled people respond to stigma reveals that they can play a significant role in managing this problem. Many may seem relatively unsophisticated and limited in the range of options that they exercise, but with help they can become competent and shrewd in the management of stigma in their lives.

Some of these strategies are not controversial and have wide support, such as covering. People who use others strategies, like passing and confronting perpetrators of stigma, may need help in considering the risks involved and learning how to do it. Seeking the "positive side" of being labeled seems to be a strategy that is often counterproductive, particularly if it thwarts efforts to become more self-sufficient.

Taking Another Personal Inventory on Stigma

In Chapter 2, I asked the reader to take a personal inventory of any biases or stereotypes that you may have pertaining to people with a mental retardation label. I would like for you to consider a few additional personal questions at this time, before proceeding to Part II.

1. Do you sometimes find yourself encouraging labeled people to be unnecessarily dependent?
2. Do you offer enough opportunities for labeled people to express themselves?
3. How do you talk about the labeled people that you know with others? How, if at all, do you refer to their disabilities?
4. Do you feel discomfort when talking to labeled people about their disabilities and stigma problems? If so, what may be some of the reasons?
5. Can you think of any new roles that you could offer labeled people that are highly valued and recognize their strengths?

References

Andron, L. (1984). The experts discuss retardation: Labeled as retarded, they now speak for themselves. Unpublished paper, Neuropsychiatric Institute, UCLA, Los Angeles, CA.

Carabello, B. (1982). Who the hell do you think that I am? In P. Williams & B. Shoultz (Eds.), *We can speak for ourselves: Self-advocacy by mentally handicapped people*, pp. 75–79. Bloomington, IN: Indiana University Press.

Dudley, J. (1983). *Living with stigma: The plight of the people who we label mentally retarded.* Springfield, Il: Charles C Thomas.

Goffman, E. (1963). *Stigma: Notes on the management of spoiled identity.* Englewood Cliffs, NJ: Prentice-Hall.

Killius, P. (1982). I can do something for you. In P. Williams & B. Shoultz (Eds.), *We can speak for ourselves: Self-advocacy by mentally handicapped people,* pp. 79–83. Bloomington, IN: Indiana University Press.

Lemert, E. (1972). *Human deviance, social problems, and social control,* 2nd ed. Englewood Cliffs, NJ: Prentice Hall.

Levine, H., & Langness, L. (1986). Conclusions: Themes in an anthropology of mild mental retardation. In L. Langness & H. Levine (Eds.), *Culture and retardation,* 191–206. Boston: D. Reidel.

Schwartz, D. (1992). *Crossing the river: Creating a conceptual revolution in community and disability.* Cambridge, MA: Brookline Books.

Wolfensberger, W. (1972). *The principle of normalization in human services.* Toronto: National Institute on Mental Retardation.

Wolfensberger, W. (1976). The origin and nature of our institutional models. In R. Kugel (Ed.). *Changing patterns in residential services for the mentally retarded,* Revised Edition. Washington, D.C.: President's Committee on Mental Retardation.

Part II
Confronting Stigma

Chapter 7

CONFRONTING STIGMA: A GENERAL APPROACH

Four guidelines are introduced in this chapter. These guidelines combine to describe a general approach to confronting stigma. The guidelines can be applied in a wide range of settings, and later chapters illustrate some of the specific ways in which they can be implemented.

The guidelines are:

1. Stigma-related problems and disability-related problems are fundamentally different and require different solutions.
2. The perpetrators of stigma are an important target of change.
3. People labeled with mental retardation should play a central role in confronting their stigma problems, with their strengths being emphasized.
4. People who are not labeled with mental retardation have a valuable role to play as "allies" in confronting stigma.

These guidelines have evolved from how I have conceptualized the problem of stigma and applied it to my work over the past 15 years. While each of my projects on stigma has been different, all have had the same overall intent—to combat stigma and promote societal inclusion for labeled people. In all of these projects, I have used a socio-anthropological perspective and have distinguished disability and stigma problems. Each project has involved labeled individuals as active participants and has attempted to influence perpetrators of stigma.

Because I am a social work educator and work in an academic setting, my projects and activities have had an academic flavor. I have usually worked in partnership with students and social agencies offering field practicums. Nonetheless, the projects that I describe in later chapters can easily be applied in all types of community agencies.

1. Stigma-Related Problems Are Not Disability-Related Problems

Typically, people view stigma problems and the challenges inherent in a disability as if they are aspects of the same problem, for they both revolve around the person with the disability. The problems amenable to a sociological solution somehow are incorrectly understood as medical or clinical problems. A danger in this tendency is that the problem area of stigma gets overlooked or is addressed as if it is a problem of the labeled person.

The disabilities of people labeled with mental retardation do, to varying degrees, impose challenges to their mental, physical, and social functioning. These disability-related challenges are the major focus of the service provisions of the mental retardation system and most of the research conducted in this field. In contrast, the problems that people have with stigma are largely overlooked and misunderstood. This happens in part because the mental retardation system does not view the problem of stigma as one of its primary targets.

My approach to confronting stigma draws its theoretical understanding primarily from sociology, social psychology, anthropology, and political science. These sciences are peripheral to most of the research and professional practice in the field of mental retardation, as the field is primarily dominated and influenced by a bio-psychological perspective (medicine, biology, and psychology). This peripheral status is partially the result of basic ideological differences between the bio-psychological and socio-anthropological perspectives on defining mental retardation. The former perspective tends to view mental retardation as a fixed biological property residing in a person, while the latter perspective views it as a property bestowed by some people upon other people because they fail to meet a social system's norms or standards (Mercer, 1973). Both perspectives have a contribution to make to this field. However, each one investigates the problems surrounding mental retardation with different values, knowledge, and intentions.

Two concepts, stigma and stigma identifiers, help illuminate why we have difficulty distinguishing stigma and disability-related problems. *Stigma* is a sociological concept. Goffman (1963) defines stigma as an undesirable social property such as a stereotype that is assigned to people when they have an attribute that deviates negatively from societal norms. Stigma becomes evident if a nondisabled person's actions resulting from holding a stereotype lead to restrictions on a labeled person's ability to develop their potential (Coleman, 1986).

For example, in the case of people with Down syndrome, stigma becomes alive in stereotypes like immaturity and childlike behavior that are incorrectly assumed to be inherent in Down syndrome. When someone believes these stereotypes, they can be overprotective of people with Down syndrome and discourage them from furthering their potential.

Stigma Identifiers are manifestations of the person's "undesirable" differentness. These identifiers can take many forms. They can be physical attributes of labeled people, their possessions, associations with other people, or affiliations with programs and organizations that attract stigma. These identifiers are an important property in stigma-promoting acts because they reveal the visible signs or cues that the person is both different from others and stigmatized.

Some attributes of Down syndrome, for example, are stigma identifiers because they attract stigma. These physical characteristics are a small nose with a low nasal bridge, upslanting eyes, fullness in the lower eyelids, and a tendency to protrude the tongue.

It is important to emphasize that stigma and stigma identifiers are not the same. Stigma takes the forms of stereotypes and myths that distort our perceptions of who a person is. Stigma identifiers are only visible cues of differentness. The problem emerges when we are not aware of our stereotypes about labeled people. In such cases, their stigma identifiers activate these stereotypes in our consciousness at some level and lead us to commit acts of stigma-promotion. Chapter 3 offers further explanation of the nature of stigma promoting acts.

2. The Goal Is to Facilitate Change in Perpetrators of Stigma

"Confronting" the people and groups who perpetrate stigma, particularly caregivers, neighbors, parents, and strangers, may pose formidable challenges. After all, caregivers do not want to be told how to do their job. Strangers, neighbors, and other acquaintances do not want to expose their biases. And family members are tired of having others tell them what to do.

"Confronting" means targeting ignorance in other people and groups. However, "confronting," in this book, does not include verbal or aggressive attacks, which can be counterproductive. The intent of "confronting" is to expose the problem in a way that everyone can understand.

Confronting the problem means to win people over to the side of the people being stigmatized. The overall strategy is for both the perpetrator and the stigmatized to have positive outcomes.

An example from my own work illustrates this point. I was giving a class presentation to a group of labeled people, and one person with a hearing impairment seemed to be inattentive. His eyes were wandering and he was yawning. I was aware that his inattentiveness was upsetting me. A short time later he asked a question about something that I had just covered. Because I felt that he had not been listening, I began to "counsel" him to keep eye contact so that he could read my lips. (I am keenly sensitive to whether or not people listen to me when I talk.) He became sullen, and I knew immediately that I had overreacted. I may have misinterpreted his inattentiveness and more importantly, I was admonishing him, albeit subconsciously, by focusing on his disability.

In retrospect, I felt embarrassed and humiliated. How could I, a "stigma expert," do such a thing. I began to think about what I could do to resolve this problem that *I had created.* I decided to meet with this person to apologize. But that was difficult for me to do. I began to make up all kinds of excuses, like rationalizing that he had probably forgotten the incident or it was not important to him. Also, I obsessed on how hard it would be to admit to what I had done. What if my colleagues and other individuals from the class would find out.

It turned out that apologizing was the right thing to do! When I brought up the issue one week later, he denied that it was important. But when I restated my apology, he angrily blurted out, "You made me feel like a retard!" I needed to hear his angry reply because I had perpetrated stigma onto him. He needed to hear from me, a person in a position of authority, that I was wrong. I became aware that I had my own prejudices and some personal issues to work on. The apology was difficult but important to make. We both gained enormously from it.

Typology of Stigma-Promotion

Chapter 3 describes numerous types of stigma promotion. Some types are communicated in interpersonal contacts initiated by individuals and others are communicated by groups, the media, organizational policies, and larger institutions. This typology infers that all different kinds of people can be promoters of stigma, including strangers, acquaintances, employers and employees, store clerks, waitresses, parents, siblings, doctors, dentists, neighbors, professional and non-professional service providers, friends, and many others. Many different types of informal and formal groups could also be stigma-promoters, including neighborhood civic groups, marriage and family counseling agencies, health clinics, family planning agencies, recreation centers, travel agencies, social clubs, church choirs, grocery stores, and countless others.

It is difficult to identify "the most serious perpetrators" of stigma in the nineties. For example, is it particular individuals or an organization? Case managers, a group home provider, the YWCA, or a community college? Each reader will need to make his or her own determination about this and set his or her own priorities for primary targets. Of course, the people labeled with mental retardation in your midst should be consulted about what these priorities should be. Most of them will be acutely aware of the most troubling sources of stigma in their lives.

Changing the Mental Retardation System

In *Living with Stigma* (Dudley, 1983), the majority of the stigma-promoting incidents that were identified involved the staff members of the mental retardation system as perpetrators. This finding was influenced by the fact that the people who were the focus of that study were consumers of this System, and they spent most of their time within this system. It would be incorrect to conclude that people working for the mental retardation system are more prone than others to promote stigma. However, the reality is that the system which has been established to help labeled people can also play a primary role in promoting stigma. Whenever this is evident, this system should be considered a major target for change.

The staff members of the mental retardation system usually choose their work out of a genuine concern for the people whom they serve. Nevertheless, they have been socialized like everyone else to believe the myths, stereotypes, and other prejudices about mental retardation and physical disabilities.

If staff members of a local mental retardation agency are a major promoter of stigma, then training programs should be instituted to help them address this problem. Training programs can be designed to expose and confront both the popular stereotypes of staff members and the misguided policies and programs of the agency. Both direct care staff and administrators can be helped to explore and analyze the origins of their problems in their previous socialization, in out-dated agency policies, and in other current and historical social forces. Further, these ill-conceived notions can be replaced by strategies that empower labeled people.

Staff members can be helped to examine their misconceptions and stigma-promoting practices through exercises as well as discussions. The "Close Association Project" in Chapter 8 and the "dyad exchanges on stigma" in chapter 11 are examples of exercises that I have used. The agency's programs and organizational structure can be evaluated as well to detect evidence of stigma. Chapter 11 offers suggestions for conducting such program evaluations.

In-service training programs focusing on caregivers in the System can, to some extent, be a prototype for designing community education programs. The attitudinal barriers of the general public may be more clearly understood vis-a-vis the attitudinal barriers of service delivery personnel. Staff and volunteers with new insights and enhanced conscientiousness about stigma can become "recovering stigma promoters" with firsthand experience and a special zeal for enlightening others. Staff members could be periodically assigned to facilitate community education workshops, co-led by labeled individuals. Chapter 11 offers examples of such workshops.

Influencing Neighborhoods, Schools, and Generic Agencies

Another important target group to consider in confronting stigma are the residents where labeled people live. These residents include not only the immediate neighbors on their block, but also local civic leaders, precinct captains, church groups, the Kiwanis Club, and other significant social units in the larger neighborhood. Among other possibilities, these nearby residents could be offered opportunities to develop friendships and other socially integrated activities with individuals having disabilities. Examples are offered in Chapter 8.

Another social group to influence are the teaching personnel and students in the local school systems, beginning at the earliest levels. The schools are one of the major institutional sources of early socialization; yet, they often need updating. Local neighborhood schools can be helped to become centers for transmitting accurate and positive information about mental retardation. Friendship exchanges between young people with and without disabilities can also be offered. To begin this process, disability professionals and self-advocacy representatives could volunteer to speak in classes and assist teachers in the design of new curriculum. Integrated classrooms should also be a priority in the schools.

A further set of organizations to target for change could be some of the generic agencies that impact on the lives of people labeled with mental retardation. These agencies may have personnel with misconceptions about disabilities and a desire to learn more effective ways of serving individuals with labels. An employment site like MacDonalds, a local YMCA or YWCA, a family planning agency, health clinic, mental health center, or marriage counseling agency are among the generic organizations that could be considered if they are either current or potential service providers.

3. Being Central Participants

Most people who are labeled with mental retardation, particularly at the mild and moderate levels, are acutely aware of their stigmatic attributes. They often reveal a keen sensitivity about their personal attributes that evoke special attention in others. In some instances they attempt to conceal these stigma identifiers, or they may practice tolerance to gain some secondary benefits from being dependent and helpless. In short, they are actors in the dramas of stigma.

Labeled people must always have the choice to become central participants in the battle against stigma. The illusion that they can be protected and sheltered from the harsh realities of stigma should not be encouraged. To the contrary, they have the most to gain from changing stigma-promoting conditions.

Moreover, we should recognize that self-determination must be respected, and many labeled people may have no desire or fortitude to get involved in confronting stigma. This is an individual decision that everyone must make for themselves. However, we must provide them with the choice. We must offer them opportunities to become involved in confronting stigma. Numerous such opportunities are described in the next five chapters.

One opportunity, peer groups, should be made available to all labeled people. While one-to-one sessions with staff and others may be helpful, peer group sessions with other labeled people can be invaluable. These groups offer opportunities for individuals to share and learn from each other, but these discussions should be reserved for the private world of labeled people. Such discussions are inappropriate to casual relationships or even everyday places like work and home.

It seems significant to note that labeled people do not freely or openly talk about their disabilities or stigma problems in the company of each other. A taboo about discussing these topics exists in many settings. Also, discussions about stereotypes can be difficult because of the humiliation of admitting to their existence. Nevertheless, avoiding these discussions only fosters even greater anguish about stigma.

These groups should be led by "allies" who are sensitive to the vulnerabilities and other difficulties that individuals face in sharing these aspects of themselves. A safe setting needs to be created and sustained for questions, feelings, and views to be openly expressed about themselves, their disabilities, and their stigma problems.

A person's disability is an important topic to explore. A disability is an important aspect of one's identity that needs to be understood in terms of what is truth and fantasy. People need to have useful individualized information about the etiology and challenges associated with their disabilities, and the extent to which the challenges can be overcome.

Another topic that needs to be explored is the mental retardation label and other labeling issues. The controversies surrounding this label needs to be brought into their world of discussion and understanding just as it has a place in professional discussions. One important question for them to explore is whether or not they perceive themselves as "mentally retarded" or even "labeled with mental retardation?" To understand their social circumstances, including the stigma aspects, they will need to have an adequate understanding of how labels are socially constructed. As stated earlier, two types of problems face labeled people, those revolving around their biopsychological disability and those having to do with the societal reaction to it. Both need to be understood. Chapter 9 covers the work of peer groups in greater depth.

Building on Their Strengths

The strengths of labeled people must be identified and affirmed if they are to succeed in confronting the stigma in their lives. A tendency in the mental retardation system is to focus on their deficits and problems, and to overlook their positive qualities.

Mount and Zwernik (1990) propose a "personal futures planning" approach to help individuals and their peers discover their strengths, personal gifts, and what they can contribute to others. In supportive groups, labeled people are helped to identify their positive qualities and potentials. Large newsprint taped to the walls is used to record many aspects of the person that may not be known to others. Some of the specific areas that can be explored in identifying strengths include the person's past experiences; a map diagraming the person's current relationships; the person's gifts, interests, and hobbies; and the person's likes and dislikes. Personal futures planning leads to dreams and images for the person's future, identified by the person within a supportive group. In this planning process, the group continues to meet to help the person put dreams into reality.

Wolfensberger (1988) reminds us of some of the types of gifts of many labeled people that are usually overlooked. Many have "heart qualities" that provide them with more mental energy for their relationships than most people have. Many have a natural and positive spontaneity of affection and interest in other people. They also have a special tendency to tap into the heart qualities of others. They can call forth gentleness, patience, and tolerance from others. Many can enjoy simple things without getting bored, and they can be direct and honest in their opinions. Obviously, not all labeled people have these qualities, but many do. In contrast, these qualities are noticeably less evident in most people without labels.

My friendships and other close relationships with different labeled people remind me of some of their gifts and qualities that I have enjoyed. Each person has been different and unique. Specifically, I have admired the loyalty that some of them have to a friend, a group, a ball team, or their country. I have enjoyed some of the topics of discussions with my friends, like dating encounters, baseball hype, intimate sharing of stigma encounters, and funny movies. I have enjoyed one friend who anticipates and quickly appreciates my jokes. She and I spend a lot of time sharing jokes and laughing together.

I have also learned from my friends, for example, how to play table pool, how to be less inhibited in dancing, and how to more exuberantly express my joy when seeing a friend. I have learned how to appreciate the simple and basic things in life like having a job, eating out, and having a friend who looks forward to getting together.

4. The Role of the Ally

Several terms have been used to identify the people who can have a special role in helping confront stigma. "Assistant," "community guide," "friend," "helper," "associate," and "ally" are among the possibilities. In this book, the term "ally" has been chosen, even though other terms could be just as appropriate (Stevens, 1996).

The "ally" is defined in the dictionary as someone who is united with another, cooperates, and is a supporter. The "ally" role has equal status with the labeled person rather than authority or control over him or her. Allies can be people with or without disabilities. The ally has a role to play, with resources to share, sensitivity and warmth to communicate, and special skills to offer in confronting stigma. An ally could also be involved as an advocate.

Not everyone is well-suited to being an ally in confronting stigma. At least four personal qualities are needed to be effective in this work. (1) Allies respect and appreciate the gifts of labeled people. (2) They believe in their capacity for friendship, achievement, and social inclusion. (3) They are good listeners and facilitators of discussion. (4) They do not depend upon recognition or receiving credit for what they do.

First, they need to be able to respect and appreciate labeled people. This requires a comfort with each individual's stigmatic attributes, such as a slow manner of responding, slurred speech, or less than age-appropriate behavior. An ally is not attracted to these attributes, but is able to accept them and see beyond them to the total person. An ally is able to discover and relish in the labeled person's gifts and strengths. Effective allies can imagine enjoying and learning something from this person. When they do get together, the ally is able to receive joy and laughter from the relationship.

Second, an ally believes in the potential of labeled people for friendship, achievement, and social inclusion. Reidy (1993) models this belief in her description of how to establish friendships with community groups. She recommends that individuals consider joining community associations like the Knights of Columbus, the Junior League, or a church choir. This process involves sensitively matching the labeled individual and the group by interests and possibilities for reciprocity.

Third, the ally is a good listener. Allies enjoy helping another person fully share themselves, their stories, dreams, silly thoughts, peculiarities, pains, and their deepest feelings and revelations. Allies can be talkative types but they may need to "soft pedal" their own stories, interests, and proposed solutions to problems.

The ally is comfortable being a behind-the-scenes kind of person who does not need credit for the success that may unfold. Instead, the ally revels in the success that radiates from the labeled individual when something happens. While allies will probably need to be very active initially in engaging and helping the person, they are able to recede into the background and be less central and important as the person takes greater charge. Allies feel comfortable when the person finds new friends and associates and no longer needs them as much.

The "ally" can have many different roles in helping labeled people. Several are described later in this book. The ally may be a *"match-maker"* who helps labeled people make friends with nondisabled people. The ally can be a *"group facilitator"* of the private work of labeled people. The ally can be an *"advisor"* or *"supporter"* to a self-advocacy group. Or the ally can be an *"advocate,"* working to eliminate stigma in the mental retardation system. Many other specific roles for the ally, while not covered in this book, are also possible.

Some Cautions

The work of confronting stigma is by no means easy. The overall goal is to overturn centuries of prejudice and misunderstanding. This involves empowering labeled people, sometimes for the first time. Equally important, it involves influencing the attitudes and behavior of others. It often means expecting people to do what they have previously felt was inappropriate or unnatural. Such things do not happen very quickly.

Preparing some labeled people to understand, manage, and confront the stigma in their lives will not be a simple undertaking. Resistance will come from some of them, their family members, staff members, and others.

Labeled people, in particular, are likely to resist changing their circumstances. Much of their socialization has taught them to accept their dependent state rather than to assert what they want and need. For example, expressing anger or criticism toward staff members or parents who stigmatize them may be a lot to expect. Also, it may not be natural for them to take a proactive rather than reactive approach to their social interactions. It could feel less stressful to leave things just the way they are; keeping the status-quo feels safe, secure, and familiar. Finally, it will not be easy to give up some of the advantages of being a compliant consumer of the mental retardation system. Staff members naturally have a greater tendency to like compliant consumers over demanding ones, and to reward them with more attention and access to opportunities.

All of these cautions add up to the point that many labeled people will likely become involved in confronting stigma very gradually and hesitantly.

Parents and other family members may also be a source of resistance in confronting stigma. Even though labeled person may not be living with their families, they may have regular contact. Parents have had the greatest impact on a labeled person's self-perception and attitudes toward stigma during childhood, and they may still have some influence. Resistance may come from parents, in part, because they will have to face the dilemma of admitting to past views and practices condoning stigma. If parents are overly protective or hesitant to support significant changes in their adult children, they may need help. Parents may need help through professional counseling, a parent's group, or other programs addressing their hesitancies and resistance.

Opposition may also come from direct care staff, supervisors and administrators, board members, volunteers, and others in the System. Direct care staff members in particular may have to do some serious soul searching before they will voluntarily make changes in their approach. At times they may be called upon to share their power with consumers, and their perspectives on what consumers are capable of thinking and doing may have to be turned upside down. Staff support groups and training sessions may need to be established to help them.

Five Ways to Confront Stigma

While there may be a multitude of ways of applying the four guidelines described in this chapter, the remaining chapters focus on the ones with which I have the most experience. Each chapter describes both projects of mine and others. Each chapter offers plenty of examples involving labeled people and allies. Detailed guidelines are also included to encourage replication in your settings.

The topics of the remaining chapters are as follows:

Chapter 8: Promoting friendships among people with and without disabilities;

Chapter 9: Facilitating the private work of labeled people in peer groups;

Chapter 10: Helping members of the self-advocacy movement;

Chapter 11: Eliminating stigma in the mental retardation system;

Chapter 12: Helping some people leave the System.

References

Dudley, J.R. (1983). *Living with stigma: The plight of the people who we label mentally retarded.* Springfield, IL: Charles C Thomas.

Coleman, L. (1986). Stigma: An enigma demystified. In S. Ainlay, G. Becker, & L. Coleman (Eds.), *The dilemma of difference: A multidisciplinary view of stigma,* pp. 211–232. New York: Plenum.

Goffman, E. (1963). *Stigma: Notes on the management of spoiled identity.* Englewood Cliffs, NJ: Prentice-Hall.

Mercer, J.R. (1973). *Labeling the mentally retarded: Clinical and social perspectives on mental retardation.* Berkeley: University of California Press.

Mount, B., & Zwernik, K. (1990). *Making futures happen: A manual for facilitators of personal futures planning.* St. Paul: Metropolitan Council.

Reidy, D. (1993). Friendship and community associations, in Amado (Ed.). *Friendships and community connections between people with and without developmental disabilities,* pp. 351–371. Baltimore: Paul H. Brooks.

Stevens, K. (1996). Karen Stevens, Ed.D., Director of The Integration Network of Western Massachusetts, offered the term, "ally."

Wolfensberger, W. (1988). Common assets of mentally retarded people that are commonly not acknowledged. *Mental Retardation,* 26(2), 63–70.

Chapter 8

PROMOTING FRIENDSHIPS AND
OTHER CLOSE ASSOCIATIONS

John and his acceptance in this town has a lesson to offer to any town because it's just a matter of . . . taking a look at the guy who walks around the corner or the lady who sits on her stoop all day long, and not looking at them as a handicapped man or a senile old lady, but looking at them as part of your town . . . (Andrews, 1995, p. 116).

A student: The most important thing about my contact with Terry is that I found a friend. And friends are one of the best things that people have . . . I have always had a wide range of friends. Some were so different than others . . . Terry has even widened that range. But most important, I can say that Terry is my friend.

A student: I feel that people who have experienced disabilities are our best teachers and should not be overlooked as a resource for learning.

A central goal in confronting stigma is for all of us to be fully accepting of people with a mental retardation label and freely including them in our everyday lives. A nonstigmatic world is one in which people with and without disabilities have mutual respect, interdependency, close associations, and friendships.

This chapter focuses on friendships and other close associations. Drawing from successful projects, the chapter describes ways to promote friendships between persons with and without a disability, and friendships that bond labeled individuals with groups of nondisabled people. Also, a project is presented that fosters close associations between students and labeled people and offers a deeper understanding of stigma.

Limited Opportunities for
Meaningful "Outside" Relationships

One measure of an inclusive society is the widespread existence of genuine friendships between people with and without disabilities. Perhaps, everyone in society who wishes to confront stigma should ask themselves,

"Do I have friends who have disabilities?" If the answer is "no," forming a friendship could be a big personal step toward overcoming stigma.

Several studies cited in Chapter 4 reveal that most people with disabilities do not have "real" friendships with nondisabled people. Their friends are most often other labeled people who are their roommates and fellow employees in sheltered settings. If they attend special clubs sponsored by a mental retardation agency, many of their friends are likely to be found there as well. Beyond these people, they may also identify their staff members as friends, but these associations are usually not considered friendships by the staff members involved. Furthermore, the time that they spend together is typically limited to the settings in which staff are paid to work with them.

In recent years, many research studies have been asking labeled people the question: "Who is your best friend?" This question typically elicits three types of responses: another labeled person, a staff member, or a person who has neither status (an "outside friend"). This question is intended, in part, to determine how many labeled people identify their best friend as an "outsider," someone who is not part of the mentally retarded world.

Some recent studies reveal that "outside friends" are often identified (e.g., Anderson, Lakin, Hill, & Chen, 1992; Dudley, Ahlgrim-Delzell, & Conroy, 1995). While these findings appear to be positive, their meaning may be misunderstood. "Outside friends" may only reflect the perception of labeled people and not the other person identified in the friendship. These associations may be more accurately defined as acquaintances or in some cases even imaginary friends. Some, however, are real and genuine.

Promoting Friendships

I am mindful of some of my own friendships with people who are labeled with mental retardation. Each of these friendships has been different in some ways. Some naturally evolved without much effort and others took considerable time and energy to develop and maintain. These friendships have lasted for short and long periods. As I have discovered the special gifts of the other person, I have wanted the relationship to grow so that common interests could be shared and enjoyed. In all cases these relationships have brought enjoyment into my life.

Some people may not need help in establishing friendships with labeled people while others will. Innovative approaches for establishing friendships have been introduced in the literature (e.g., Perske, 1988; Taylor, Bogdan, & Lutfiyya, 1995). One outstanding contribution is a book entitled *Friendships and Community Connections Between People with and Without Developmental Disabilities* (Amado, 1993a). A philosophical position of this book is that these friendships are vital to both the individuals involved and the community as a whole.

Amado (1993a) points out that the mental retardation system is not usually effective in promoting friendships between their consumers and others in their community. Actually, the System seems to largely ignore any responsibility for fostering such interdependence (Newton, Olson, & Horner, 1995). At times the System even inadvertently discourages such friendships by the various ways that it controls its consumers' daily lives.

Interdependence can be discovered when the System opens its consumers' doors to activities with all kinds of people, particularly opportunities in which they can contribute as well as receive. The System needs to do more to encourage consumers to partake in a variety of new relationships, including seeking new companions in their neighborhoods, and having more frequent contact with family members, church members, and others where they work. Providers should be focusing more of their resources on assisting consumers in creating and sustaining these new relationships.

According to Amado (1993a), bridges must be created to community life in general, with the community being more than the immediate neighborhood. Connections should be encouraged with people wherever they have something to offer, and this requires that considerations be given to a wide range of groups.

Steps Involved in Establishing Friendships: "Allies" who intend to foster new friendships between people with and without disabilities are likely to follow several general principles (Amado, 1993b). Initially, they get to know the person with a disability, including the person's desires, strengths, interests, and challenges.

Next, allies make connections with other people and groups in the community that may fit this person's interests. Exploration may involve looking for potential welcoming places where the person could contribute to and become known in a group in some way. Welcoming places could be found almost anywhere, for example, coffee clubs, exercise groups, or prayer groups. Once welcoming groups are found, individual people in these groups are identified who might be interested in becoming friends with a person with a disability.

Once a possible match is discovered, making introductions logically comes next. The gifts, strengths, and interests of the individual are identified in the introduction, and their disability is introduced in a way that facilitates the relationship. No more needs to be said about the disability beyond what will help facilitate a new relationship. Labels and other stigmatizing information are not helpful.

Finally, support may be needed in the ongoing development of these relationships, including their ups and downs. The ally can have periodic contact with labeled people to find out how things are going, to support them in unfamiliar areas of developing a friendship, and to offer assistance when possible misunderstandings or differences arise in the friendship. For example, a labeled individual may want more frequent contact with a new friend and is not sure how to both communicate this need and tune into the other person's needs.

Matching a Person with a Group: Reidy (1993) describes an approach in matching labeled people with informal community groups. She offers principles that are similar to the steps in building dyad relationships. After getting to know the person with a disability, the ally finds a compatible group in the community. Next, the ally gets well acquainted with this group. In this process, the ally and individual should consider what characteristics of the group fit well with him or her and what characteristics do not.

One of Reidy's examples is a match between Dee, who has a disability, and an Evening Walking Group. Dee is similar in age and physical characteristics to the others in the group. Her pace of walking and endurance level matches that of the group. Even though Dee has limited communication abilities and a stubborn personality, she is fully accepted by the group members. The match was worked out by an ally who is an occasional member of the group.

An ally may need to stay involved long enough to facilitate the development of the match. The ally, for example, may pay attention to specific issues like assisting in getting the person to the group, helping in obtaining membership, and pointing out the special rituals and routines of the group. Sometimes the ally should attend a few meetings with the individual until some of the initial adjustments are made.

The individual with a disability may also need help in getting to know some members. Introductions are needed that point out common characteristics and mention the person's disability issues in a way that fosters connection. An example is given of Joan's introduction to her group (Reidy, p. 365, 1993). The introduction used was, "Joan has some difficulties communicating with words, but she is very capable of making herself understood," rather than "Joan has mild M.R., is nonverbal, and uses total communication to get her needs across." Other important considerations in the introduction include asking the individual how she wants to be introduced, and emphasizing her strengths and capabilities rather than her disability challenges.

Most important, the individual may need help in becoming a valuable contributing member. Dee, who was mentioned in the earlier example, often pushes the stroller of one member's granddaughter when they walk. Not only did this role relieve the older member of this task but also led to Dee talking more as they walked. In becoming a contributing member, Dee felt more comfortable sharing herself with the other walkers.

Reidy recommends that the ally should also keep some ongoing contact with the group to assist when difficulties arise and to facilitate ways for the individual to become more active and contributing.

Examples of Successful "Outside" Relationships

The recent literature suggests that a significant number of labeled people in society *do have* meaningful friendships and other rewarding social relationships outside the "mentally retarded world." Much can be learned about what makes these relationships work.

Taylor, Bogdan, and Lutfiyya (1995) present a collection of stories about people with disabilities who have formed friendships in their communities. These stories illustrate how beneficial these friendships can become for everyone who is involved.

One example is a man named John who moves to a new small town after living a very isolated life in large city (Andrews, 1995). John rather quickly becomes pals with a rock-and-roll drummer. He begins spending time with his pal in clubs and meets other people, often on the dance floor. Later, he begins taking art lessons. He discovers that he has some special artistic talents and he ends up having an art show of his own. Meanwhile, a couple of part-time jobs also come his way. John's brother, sums up this experience by saying,

John and his acceptance in this town has a lesson to offer to any town because it's just a matter of where you live and where you're at—taking a look at the guy who walks around the corner or the lady who sits on her stoop all day long, and not looking at them as a handicapped man or a senile old lady, but looking at them as part of your town. And if any community allows its members to be individuals, then someone like John . . . is going to be loved and accepted (Andrews, 1995, p. 116).

Taylor and Bogdan (1989) have flipped the analysis from the traditional study of deviance and its malaise of segregation and isolation, to a new sociology of acceptance. Their interest is in studying experiences in friendship and societal inclusion that work, rather than studying what does not work.

Taylor and Bogdan focus on "accepting relationships," which they define as

a relationship between a person with a deviant attribute such as mental retardation and a non-disabled person, which is long-standing and characterized by closeness and affection and in which the deviant attribute, or disability, does not have a stigmatizing, or morally discrediting character in the eyes of the non-disabled person (1989, p. 27).

Through qualitative studies of cases of accepting relationships, they have discovered a range of sentiments and motivations for why nondisabled people choose these relationships. Four major motivations were identified from their case studies, including a family commitment, a religious calling, a humanitarian concern, and feelings of friendship. The last motivation is distinguished from the others in that it is based on liking and enjoying the company of the person with a disability, while the others are based more on abstract values.

Diversity Issues: A fifth major motivation for choosing relationships with labeled people should also be considered—cultural values. Some ethnic cultures have been found to be more accepting of their members with deviant attributes than the majority white culture (e.g., Edgerton, 1984; Henshel, 1972). Unfortunately, few studies have focused on how such cultural groups have fostered accepting relationships with their labeled members.

Edgerton (1989) refers to labeled people in these cultures as the "hidden majority" of people labeled with mild levels of mental retardation. These people may have had a mental retardation diagnosis during their school years but not as adults. Often they are part of the lower socioeconomic strata and from racial minority groups. Many of these people appear to be fairly well integrated in their cultural subgroups in society.

Much can be learned from accepting relationships between people with and without disabilities. Future research should examine the power of values in a community, whether they be based on family, religion, humanitarianism, or a cultural group. For example, is acceptance of labeled people more evident in particular religious communities? If so, how could these religious values be replicated by other groups. Also, is acceptance of labeled people more likely in an African American cultural group than a Caucasian one? If so, is acceptance more likely to exist because its members can understand the stigma associated with a disability based on their own personal experiences with stigma?

It is important to note that the mental retardation system has seldom been identified in studies as a model for facilitating accepting relationships. One exception may be a special service provider such as L'Arche communities in which people with and without disabilities live together as equals (Vanier, 1979). Yet, religious values, not professional ones, seem to explain the philosophy driving L'Arche. Other exceptions are many citizen advocacy agencies and community education groups that work in the disability field. These groups often assume an important role in promoting accepting relationships within and outside the mental retardation service system.

We need to learn more about the qualities of accepting relationships. Taylor and Bogdan (1989) identify some of these qualities. They state that becoming friends with a person having a disability is "a process in which the person essentially becomes 'delabeled'" (Taylor & Bogdan, 1989, p. 32). While the deviant attributes are prominent in the early stages of the relationship, these aspects diminish in importance over time.

Other positive qualities of the labeled person become central as the friendship builds. Over time, the relationship becomes a reciprocal one in which both people give and receive to each other. For example, one person without a disability states:

> I really like spending time with him. Why? Because we both have active imaginations, are artistic, share the same sense of humor, love chocolate, and like good coffee on Sunday mornings. We both like to cook good meals and listen to jazz . . . That's why we're such good friends. (Taylor & Bogdan, 1989, p. 32)

Understanding Stigma Through
a Close Association: A Project

Many of the qualities in the friendships described above are also important in relationships between staff members and their consumers. For example, acceptance is paramount to a successful staff/consumer relationship. Also, staff members must see beyond their consumers' disability attributes to the whole person in order to truly help them.

As was pointed out earlier in the book, many staff members are largely unaware of the stigma problems of their consumers and could be perpetrators of stigma. An important question to ask is why more attention has not been given to addressing this problem.

For many years, I have offered a project to university students as part of a professional course on developmental disabilities (Dudley, 1995). The project involves each student in a "personal association" with a labeled person. I refer to the labeled person as an "associate." I work closely with the students and a group of social agencies to arrange and support these associations.

The purpose of the project is to promote mutual understanding and possible friendship between the student and a person labeled with mental retardation. I began this project because I have found that students preparing to work in the human service field have seldom had any prior meaningful contacts with labeled people. Like most people, they hold a number of familiar stereotypes and are largely unaware of the stigma issues addressed in this book. One student's comments, after being introduced to the project, is an example:

> After talking about the project, I was getting many "ideas" about people with mental retardation flying around my brain—too many categories and labels and exceptions and statements like, "Oh, but their most loveable, warm people." I was really on edge—and wanted to get out and be with my associate, meet him, play games and talk with him myself—perhaps wanting to destroy ideas that are labeled and categorized with words.

Another student's comments are also revealing,

> This is the first time I have ever had direct contact with mentally retarded persons. Before this time the major contact I had with the label "retarded" was from my older brother who used to call me "retarded" when I was small because I had a overbite and wore glasses. Other than that I haven't had much contact.

The intent of this "personal association" is to provide students with an experiential opportunity in which their own stereotypes are exposed and confronted. Also, they are helped to discover that a labeled person could have much in common with them. Furthermore, this opportunity is intended to offer a possible new friendship with a person having a disability.

The timing of this project is important, coming before these students enter the human service system as professional caregivers. The project helps them to perceive labeled people as individuals, not by stereotypes, and to recognize each person's strengths. Students are also helped to examine the stigma problems faced by their associate. This personal association provides than with a firsthand exposure to the stigma encountered every day by one individual.

Guidelines in Implementing the Project

The project is driven by several guidelines that have evolved through experience. With modifications, these guidelines can be applied in several different settings, including social agencies, college and university settings, secondary schools, churches and synagogues, private clubs, and neighborhood associations. The guidelines that follow will need to be applied flexibly, based on the circumstances of the people involved in your project.

1. The Matching Process Is Critical: I always carefully match the students with their personal associates. I have become aware of several issues that need to be considered to maximize the chances of a successful relationship and to avoid some of the typical pitfalls.

Overall, I have matched two people with as few potential barriers as possible to maximize the likelihood that they will make a successful connection. I have found that matching people similar in age and of the same gender and race makes it easier for them to initially discover their common interests.

I have found that mixing an older and younger person adds the perception (or misperception) of differences in interests, energy, and values that may impede the relationship. Matching a man and women adds a sexual element that may be confusing to the person with a disability (e.g., the student may be perceived as a potential romantic partner). Racial differences, while offering another important aspect of diversity to the relationship, tend to also add another potential barrier in the beginning.

Sometimes, I match people by interests. I have matched, for example, a student and associate when both were married or seriously dating, and when both liked the same activities, such as bowling, skating, or going to ball games. Also, shopping at the mall has been the basis for a match.

I have usually restricted the "associates" to people labeled with mild or moderate levels of retardation. My reasoning has been that there are numerous people at the higher levels of functioning who desperately want friendships or more socially inclusive experiences. Also, I feel that students without prior experience in this field have an easier time discovering their commonality with someone with a milder disability and more developed social skills.

I have involved a more diverse group of people with disabilities as well. At times, I have involved people with severe disabilities if they are interested in a close association and are sponsored by an agency, and if a student is available who has had some experiences with people with disabilities.

2. Involving a Sponsoring Agency Helps: I usually work with social agencies that provide leisure, recreational, or residential services to labeled people. With agency involvement, people with disabilities can initially have a staff member helping them decide whether or not to participate.

An agency representative is asked to either announce this program to their consumers or to individually select possible candidates. I ask sponsoring agencies and their consumers to consider a number of important questions in deciding who should participate. Can this labeled person benefit from such an association? What could be gained from such a relationship? How has this person handled short-term relationships in the past? Could a short-term relationship that will not continue beyond 14 weeks cause harm or major disappointment? Has this person previously had "outside" relationships? Have these experiences been positive or have they been disappointing and possibly harmful?

An agency sponsor can also be valuable in providing basic identifying information about the associate that will help the student in the initial stages. This information includes special strengths, like a special sense of humor or an ability to drive a car. Also, selected information about the associate's disability can be helpful, such as understanding their physical limitations on a shopping excursion or the extent that they can travel on public transportation by themselves. Labels and other diagnostic information are usually not provided.

The agency sponsor is available if problems arise and consultation is needed by the student. For example, difficulties sometimes arise around the last three or four weeks of the experience. The student and associate are encouraged to discuss the ending of their relationship, including what they have enjoyed and how they feel about ending. Sometimes, the sponsoring agency can assist the associate in working through ending feelings and, if appropriate, finding other people or supports to take the student's place.

Initially, all of the students and associates are told that the relationship will only occur during the semester. If both parties decide on their own to continue to have contact after the project is over, the specific arrangements need to be clearly understood and agreed upon by both people. Likewise, if either the student or associate do not wish to continue the relationships after the semester is completed, this decision needs to be clearly understood and honored. Typically, about 3 or 4 students in a class of 25 and their personal associates decide to continue an active friendship. Others maintain some phone contact for awhile and occasionally get together.

3. Friend and Helper Roles Can Be in Conflict: I inform my students that their relationship with their associate should be as equals, and it should not involve a helping role. I have found that it is fairly easy for these students to automatically "take on" the helper role with a labeled person or at least to communicate caregiving messages.

A student illustrates,

> I noticed myself watching other people's reactions to Nora while we were out. (I guess I just assumed people would react to her differently.) I felt myself really feeling defensive. I'm wondering if the defensiveness on my part stems from the attitude that Nora is vulnerable?

This strong tendency to be the helper raises some important issues that are often discussed in class. Stereotypes are often discussed such as the tendency to presume that labeled people are dependent, helpless, and in need our assistance. I often remind the students that these people receive professional services from the human service system, but seldom have significant "outside" relationships like these personal associations.

A student who caught herself attempting to be a helper serves as an example of how this role can get in the way:

> Paula shared with me that she was moving to a group home. I asked her how she felt about the exciting news? Paula's response was, "I don't want to move, I want to move to my mother's house." My response, nonverbal, was "How am I going to deal with this?" I have become so accustomed to knowing the proper procedures in dealing with situations like this that I drew a blank. Reorganizing my thoughts,

I realized that first, she is not my client . . . Second, how would I respond to a friend in a similar situation?

Many of my students are no different from others in our society who are isolated from labeled people; they have not previously had close friendships with labeled people and do not feel confident of their ability to function in such relationships. In large part, their own stereotypes and other biases are likely to preclude a normal relationship from occurring. Thus, I operate from the assumption that an accepting relationship between the student and labeled person needs to be learned.

I ask my students to model the relationship after one of their other friendships. A primary objective of this relationship is for the student to learn more about the personal life of the associate—his or her hobbies, work, friends, dating, and favorite activities or outings. Conversely, the students are encouraged to share their own personal life as well—their school routines, hobbies, dating experiences, etc.

Students are reminded to consider the power issues in the relationship and the likelihood that both parties will perceive that the student is more powerful (O'Brien & O'Brien, 1993). To develop a balanced relationship, students are reminded that their associates may need some encouragement to openly express themselves, volunteer a topic for discussion, or choose an activity to do together. Otherwise, the associate may "fall into" a more familiar dependent, acquiescent role. Likewise, the students are asked not to dominate discussions with their favorite topics or to only show interest in activities that they want to do; they are also encouraged not to withhold their preferences altogether. Students are also discouraged from challenging the views of the associate, particularly in the early stages of the relationship.

4. Learning About Stigma Issues: A central purpose of the project is to help students become acquainted with the stigma problems of their associates. I usually help them to examine several areas of concern related to stigma. First, I ask them to become aware of the stigmatic attributes of their associate. I ask the student to consider the impact that these attributes may have on them; specifically, I ask the students to be aware of any stereotypes and biases that they may have. Second, I ask them to become aware of and sensitive to the role of stigma in their associate's life, particularly as it may be revealed in discussions or common activities. When stigma issues arise, I encourage the students to sensitively enter into these discussions. Third, I ask them to observe acts of stigma-promotion while they are with their associate. Finally, I ask them to be aware of how their associate responds to and manages these stigma-promoting incidents. These topics are elaborated on below.

Awareness of the impact of stigmatic attributes: One aspect of the learning process is for the students to become aware of how their associate's stigmatic attributes affect them. Students are asked to examine their feelings and to become aware of possible stereotypes or other biases that they may have.

Many class discussions are used to discuss their personal reactions to their associate and to explore the sources of these reactions. By having these discussions, the students are helped to set aside possible barriers to becoming closer to their associate, and to recognize that they could unknowingly be promoters of stigma.

A few examples of students' comments pertaining to their associates' attributes follow.

> On the bus coming home, this guy got on the bus with a big red spot of ointment on his face. Ken (my associate) asked what it was and kept looking at him. This isn't really the significant part. This man was talking to himself and I noticed the woman near him moved her packages so it seemed they wouldn't be near this man. I thought to myself this man is more stigmatized than Ken because he was talking to himself though Ken's vocabulary is not much. I thought that was interesting.

Another example of awareness of attributes,

> People invariably notice Bonnie's slight speech problem (her voice is a bit nasal due to slightly protruding front teeth) but they speak to her as they would any other adult and simply ask her to repeat herself if they're unsure of what she said. Her slightly abnormal speech is really the only stigma symbol that she has and that is not even very stigmatic.

A third student revealed his keen sensitivity to stigmatic attributes,

> My first impression (of my associate) was that he was very different from the other people with mental retardation I had met. I believe that he may be classified as "borderline." Physically, he looks like many other 21-year-olds, that is, he has no gross physical features that would make him seem retarded. He does look a little boyish though, but then so do I.

Another student shared her discomfort about her associate's attributes,

> (While shopping) Ann began trying on a dress. While trying it on, she began talking very loudly and said over and over that she had to buy deodorant because the other clients stole hers. I noticed other people in the dressing room area began

starring at me. (I was outside her curtain.) I would say that her loud talking and her repeating of the same thing are stigma identifiers (that bothered me).

The course is used to explore numerous stereotypes that students may have internalized about people labeled with mental retardation. Students often become aware of their stereotypes as they interact with their associate.

One stereotype that usually comes up initially is that their associates will not be able to carry on a decent or interesting conversation with them. I usually only respond that the students should be good listeners, and give attention to encouraging their associate to talk.

After spending some initial time with their associates, the students confront this stereotype head on, as the following student did,

> . . . I had always been led to believe that even adults with mild retardation had no real sensitivity toward others and had no idea of how to do such things as try to put others to ease. I'm beginning to realize how ignorant I've been where Joanne is concerned.

Another comments,

> . . . These are manifestations of the "normality" of Tasha's thoughts, perceptions, and actions. She notices nice-looking men, fusses over her own appearance, and teases people just like anyone else her age and sex does. I'm still amazed at my ignorance about mental retardation and the difficulty with which I'm letting go of misconceptions.

Discussing stigma issues: I encourage the students to be prepared to sensitively discuss the stigma issues of their associate if such issues are brought up by the associate. For example, if an associate is angry because a waitress ignored her when taking an order, the student is encouraged to be supportive of the associate's feelings and open to the associate's desire for further discussion of this incident.

The topic of labels is a frequently mentioned stigma topic, e.g., the associates may say that they are not "a retard" or they are very different from others in their presence who have more stigmatic attributes. A student illustrates,

> Bill said that he has to hide his possessions when he returns to (agency) where he lives because the residents would steal them. I asked him further about this and he said that he has a lot of things taken by other residents. He further stated that he doesn't belong there with "all of these retarded people." I thought this would be a good opportunity to explore how Bill views himself. I remembered that he had earlier said that his father told someone that he has "a good head on his shoulders." I asked him what he meant when he said that he did not belong with

retarded people? . . . I then hesitantly asked if he thought of himself as mentally retarded? He said adamantly, "No!" I asked what he did think, and he replied very confidently, "normal." . . . However, his behavior seems to indicate that he actually does perceive himself as different. He says that a group home is needed (by him) so he can learn how to live in the community. I think moving into a group home and living in the community is more "normal" to him than being in an institution.

Another student shares a vivid example of his associate's sensitivity to labels,

We talk a lot about John's feelings about stigma and some people's reactions to the retarded. John said a very interesting thing to me the other night. He said, "It's a shame they can't get a knife and cut the retardation out." It says to me just how thick his self-concept is full of these attitudes toward himself as being retarded and others' attitudes as well—if only we could 'cut' that part out.

Observing stigma-promotion: Students are asked to be aware of stigma-promoting incidents involving their associate, and they frequently observe such incidents while they are spending time together. One student's example:

Three guys on a bus were making fun of Marna when she wasn't looking and I heard one of them calling her a "retard." Marna asked me later on what to do the next time that this happened? After some discussion, I asked Marna how she felt when they called her that name? She said it hurt her feelings because it wasn't true, she was just a "slow learner."

Often students observe someone staring at their associate while they were out in a public place. An example,

We sat down at a table next to an older man with two young children. As we ate, I noticed this man was staring at Janine. When he noticed that I saw him looking, he looked away. However, a few minutes later, he began staring at her again. Janine didn't seem to notice that she was being watched and she continued to talk about various things.

Students also observe staff members who work in the residential and work settings of their associates promoting stigma. An example:

Randy's discussion of the time-out procedure at (agency) was especially interesting. It reflected how he feels like a child and also sometimes as something other than a human being. I've witnessed some of the staff's behavior while waiting for Randy and it is often inappropriate and sometimes disgusting. I've seen staff members make a spectacle out of unusual behavior exhibited by a client. Some talk to the clients as if they are children and talk about the client right in front of them as if they could not hear or understand. Other workers seem indifferent to working there.

Observing patterns of coping with stigma: Students are expected to observe how their associate copes with stigma. Associates' coping strategies are often identified by students once they become aware that their associates have varying degrees of sophistication in this area. The students are helped to simply understand these patterns without needing to rescue their associate. The intent is for the student to gain insight and sensitivity about the private world of someone who is stigmatized and how they cope with this aspect of their lives. One student's example,

> At times I feel like Cary is trying to "pass." (I notice) her quietness, especially in public places, except in restaurants where she can't be heard. The time in Pizza Hut when I got verbal with the guy across from us and she didn't. Maybe she didn't want to draw attention to herself. Or on the bus, when she imitated the woman reading. Maybe she was trying to do a normal thing or imitate so she would appear normal. I realize that because of her appearance, she can pass. I honestly believe that she knows she can too. I feel this way because she tries so hard to be "normal" with her hair, clothing, etc.

Another example,

> Susie can't count. So when she orders food, she doesn't buy a large quantity. Then she won't overspend. If Susie is wrong about something, she won't admit it but she will apply her idea to another issue when she will be right.

5. The Dilemma of Requiring These Associations: This project is a requirement of students in a university course. This can be problematic because some students perceive that they are being "forced" to develop these relationships. This issue has been a popular topic of class discussions many times.

During the first two years of the project, I incorrectly described the relationship as a "friendship" to be developed between the student and labeled person. My students reminded me that friendships must be voluntary, so I renamed these relationships "personal associations," with the potential of leading to a friendship.

Inevitably, a few students argue for "rescuing" the labeled person from considering such an association. When asked to elaborate, students often say that labeled people have already been hurt enough by other people who come and go in their lives; we should not compound this problem by offering another such relationship.

This argument often launches us into fruitful discussions about whether or not we are communicating a stereotype about labeled people. I admit to the students that short-term, prearranged relationships are not ideal; yet, they may be the only opportunity for many labeled people to have an association with an "outside person." I remind the students that their relationships with consumers during their field internships are also short-term. I also ask them if they think that the people with whom they will establish associations are too fragile or "too disabled" to benefit from such a short-term association?

I often emphasize that we need to reflect on the strengths of labeled people. I remind them that the project has the built-in safeguards of an informed consent arrangement that explains to a labeled person what this association is all about before they choose to participate. Also, a sponsoring agency is involved that knows the labeled person as a consumer. This agency works behind the scenes in helping to select labeled people, clarifying the project's objectives, and monitoring the effects.

Inevitably, these discussions have led many students to admit that they were resisting this project because of some of *their own* misgivings. They mention feeling fearful, awkward, and incapable of developing such an association.

Admittedly, a voluntary project would be preferred. However, a voluntary project offered through a university course would not have reached many students. Several hundred students have been participants in this project during the past 15 years, including students in social work, psychology, special education, and other disciplines. Possibly a persuasive argument could be made for requiring all students interested in the disabilities field to develop a personal association with a person having a disability. An alternative could be to offer the "associate" experience as one of several options.

6. Reflecting Upon the Experience Afterward Is Important: The associates are informally interviewed after the experience is over to identify the benefits and possible concerns or problems. The associates are usually asked several open-ended questions by the sponsoring agency, including: how do you feel about the student and the experience, what did you like the most and least, how did you feel when the experience ended, have you heard from the student since the semester was over, and would you like to do it again if another opportunity arises?

The responses of the "associate" have generally been very positive but limited in what they reveal. A few examples of responses made by the associates are as follows:

- This was a good experience because maybe someday I'll meet other people.
- Would like to go shopping again. Go to restaurants. Meet (the student's) friends.

- I am disappointed that we will not see each other again.
- Felt good. She was nice to talk to.
- (If I had it over again) I would keep the same person and go to different places.
- I was driven around town a lot, downtown, etc. She (student) never got mad.
- Nice to do things with another person. I like going out shopping and to change . . . to go out biking if possible.
- She's nice but too "high" for me. Too hard to understand and too fast when she talks.
- I learned to not be afraid and to go out and do things.
- Enjoyed talking to someone close to my age.
- I would like to meet new people all the time instead of seeing the same people at the workshop.

The project has also been very useful to most of my students. The students are expected to keep journals of their experience, and to identify in their journals what they have learned from their associates. A sampling of journal excerpts follows.

One student shared how much she had learned as she commented about the capacity of her associate to face the stigma in her life,

> Overall, the experience has given me the opportunity to better appreciate the problems and needs of a person labeled mentally retarded. Joan shared her feelings openly about how she felt living at (institution). . . . It gave me a better idea of what living in an institution must really be like. Also, that clients labeled with mental retardation do have an awareness of how poorly they are treated and are concerned about it. . . . I also had the opportunity to observe the public's reactions to a person with mental retardation. The reactions stem from staring, negative looks, patronizing her, treating her like she was a child to downright rudeness. Joan seems to keep a wall up when we go out to public places. She doesn't seem to pay much attention to people (except small children). She seems to close them out when they stare at her, and although I can't tell by any outward sign that she does realize that she is being stared at, I feel she is aware of it.

And another student confronted a stereotype of hers:

> I can remember pushing Jill to talk and her just not talking much. Maybe had I not pushed so much in the beginning she would have opened up a lot sooner. I learned a lot about accepting people as they are and not trying to change them because I feel uncomfortable. Instead, I realize that everyone is different and I have to accept the difference if I am to get to know these people better. I realize that these people are not china dolls that break. In fact, considering all the things that Jill has been through, she is a tough person. She isn't hurt as easily as I suspected. She gives the initial reaction of being hurt, but it doesn't last long.

Another student revealed some of his biases and some introspective learning:

I have unconsciously, I suppose, had some misconceptions about people who are labeled "mentally retarded," and I have greatly underestimated their awareness and their capabilities. I'm still not completely free of these things, but I do feel that I am making steady progress toward that end. I also feel that people who have experienced disabilities are our best teachers and should not be overlooked as a resource for learning.

Another student shared something that many students discover—how much she personally had in common with her associate:

The next statement may not sound right—I learned how normal people with mental retardation are. What I mean is that people with mental retardation have feelings like everyone else, bad times and good times, and the experiences that any other person would have. I have learned that people with mental retardation are just that—PEOPLE first, people with mental retardation second. That is the most important thing that I have learned.

7. Friendship Is One Possible Outcome: As I mentioned earlier, most of my students and their associates decide to either continue only occasional or sporadic telephone contact after the course experience is over or discontinue seeing each other altogether. Yet, a small number of students in each course continue their relationship with their associate indefinitely, developing a genuine friendship that takes on a life of its own. Characteristics of friendships are evident in the following examples,

As I focus on the highpoints and what I have learned from this experience, what comes to mind first is the overall enjoyment both Marna and I got out of getting to know each other and sharing different activities together. It really felt more like a friendship than an arranged assignment. We have truly enjoyed each others company and the times that we spend together, regardless of the "prearranged" beginning.

Another example,

The last few times with Sonny have been extra comfortable. Perhaps (this is) because I don't feel sorry for him and I don't think about what I'm going to say so that I don't offend him as in the beginning.

Another example,

The most important thing about my contact with Terry is that I found a friend. And friends are one of the best things that people have. The best time was when Terry and I were on the way home from getting pizza. What happened was we were sitting on a bus and she suddenly put her arms around me and gave me a kiss on the cheek and said "I like you." This meant so much to me. It is one of those times that I will never forget... I have always had a wide range of friends.

Some were so different than others they just could not get along. Terry has even widened that range. But most important I can say that Terry is my friend.

This is an important comment to consider in closing this chapter— *"Terry is my friend."* The chapter has introduced varied ways to foster friendships between people with and without disabilities. The student project is different from the others in that it is a course requirement and focuses on professional development issues. Ideally, friendship projects are voluntary and freely chosen.

People who are considering employment in the disability field may benefit from a "personal association" with a labeled person as part of their preparation. University faculty working in professional programs and trainers and supervisors in developmental disabilities agencies may want to consider such a project to help students and staff members prepare themselves to be more effective allies of labeled people.

References

Anderson, J., Lakin, K., Hill, B., & Chen, T. (1992). Social integration of older people with mental retardation in residential facilities. *American Journal on Mental Retardation*, 96(5), 488–501.

Andrews, S. (1995). Life in Mendocino: A young man with Down syndrome in a small town in Northern California. In Taylor, S., Bogdan, R., & Lutfiyya, Z. (Eds.), (1995). *The variety of community experiences: Qualitative studies of family and community life* (pp. 101–116). Baltimore: Paul H. Brookes.

Amado, A. (Ed.). (1993a). *Friendships and community connections between people with and without developmental disabilities.* Baltimore: Paul H. Brookes.

Amado, A. (1993b). Steps for reporting community connections. In Amado, A. (Ed.). *Friendships and community connections between people with and without developmental disabilities,* pp. 299–326. Baltimore: Paul H. Brookes.

Dudley, J.R. (1995). Associate Project: Introducing students to the stigma in their clients' lives. Unpublished manuscript.

Dudley, J., Ahlgrim-Delzell, L., & Conroy, J. (1995). Investigating the satisfaction of *Thomas S.* class members in year 1 & 2: Intermediate findings of two subgroups of class members with and without implemented plans, Monograph 5, Charlotte, NC: *Thomas S.* Longitudinal Research Project, August, 1995.

Edgerton, R. (Ed.), (1984). *Lives in process: Mildly retarded adults in a large city.* Washington, D.C.: American Association on Mental Retardation.

Edgerton, R.B. (1989). Retarded people of adult years. *Psychiatric Annals,* 19(4), 205–210.

Henshel, A. (1972). *The forgotten ones: A sociological study of Anglo and Chicano retardates.* Austin: University of Texas Press.

Newton, J., Olson, D., & Horner, R. (1995). Factors contributing to the stability of social relationships between individuals with mental retardation and other community members. *Mental Retardation,* 33(6), 383–393.

O'Brien, J. & O'Brien, C. (1993). Unlikely alliances: Friendships and people with developmental disabilities. In Amado, A. (Ed.). *Friendships and community connections between people with and without developmental disabilities.* Baltimore: Paul H. Brookes.

Perske, R. (1988). *Circle of friends: People with disabilities and their friends enrich the lives of one another.* Nashville: Abingdon Press.

Reidy, D. (1993). Friendship and community associations, In Amado (Ed.). *Friendships and community connections between people with and without developmental disabilities,* pp. 351–371. Baltimore: Paul H. Brookes.

Taylor, S.J., & Bogdan, R. (1989). On accepting relationships between people with mental retardation and nondisabled people: Toward an understanding of acceptance. *Disability, Handicap, & Society,* 4(1), 21–36.

Taylor, S., Bogdan, R., & Lutfiyya, Z. (Eds.), (1995). *The variety of community experiences: Qualitative studies of family and community life* (pp. 175–192). Baltimore: Paul H. Brookes.

Vanier, J. (1979). *Community and growth: Our pilgrimage together.* New York: Paulist Press.

Chapter 9

PRIVATE WORK

My friends and I want to get together to do more than bowl, dance, run a race, or watch T.V. We want to talk about our lives and what we need. We want to feel close to each other. We want to make decisions that effect our lives (Edwards, 1982, p. 68).

You know what I found out? It's consumers helping consumers. You see, a lot of people go to school to learn this. But we have the true experience, because we know what they are and what they feel. It's really true. Even the teacher at Sonoma State Hospital in 1959 said that people opened up a lot more when I took over once in awhile (Williams & Shoultz, 1982, p. 75).

Every socially oppressed group has a need to do "private work." Private work involves understanding the nature of one's oppression and finding ways to become liberated from it. The oppression that people with disabilities experience is the stigma that adversely affects their lives.

An important aspect of private work is consciousness-raising. People who are oppressed must understand the nature of their oppressive conditions, particularly if they intend to change these conditions. The women's movement is often referred to as a "consciousness-raising" movement. A woman's consciousness has been raised as she has reconsidered her values, views, and circumstances that have been derived from her socialization in a gender-biased society. People with disabilities need help as well in reconsidering their values, viewpoints, and circumstances (Szivos & Griffiths, 1990). The discovery that the responsibility for being stigmatized does not lie with themselves can be very empowering in itself (Coleman, 1986).

Private work also leads to action against oppressive conditions. Once the origins and perpetrators of oppression are understood, individual and collective ways of confronting and overcoming these conditions can more freely follow. Private work leads to relief and resolution of painful and debilitating circumstances.

Privacy and Outsiders

The work that needs to be done is private. This means that the work at hand should not be interfered with by "outsiders" who may have conflicting or competing motives. An outsider could be anyone who has not experienced this oppression. Outsiders do not have a first-hand understanding of the emotional impact of stigma and thus have less personally at stake in overcoming this oppressive problem.

Outsiders may benefit from keeping a status-quo arrangement that is oppressive. For example, outsiders could be employees of the mental retardation system who want to improve their consumers' lives but not necessarily free them of their dependent status. Family members could be outsiders who want their disabled family member to grow up and be more independent, but only to the extent that serious risks can be avoided. Other people can be outsiders who express a willingness to have labeled people participate in society, but they do not welcome them to live on their block, join their clubs, or work with them.

An "ally" is someone who can help with private work. An ally is likely to be an outsider as well. However, allies are people who can put aside their own interests and fully devote themselves to the interests of labeled people.

Group as a Mutual Aid System

Private work can be most effectively carried out in small groups with peers. Peer support groups provide unique opportunities for people to support and learn from each other. These groups are especially beneficial when people have common needs or "shared stress" (Gibbons, 1986). Stigmatized people often feel more relaxed in groups with other stigmatized peers because the group offers a respite from the role pressures that they must face in society. In these groups, people can present more of a "natural face."

Many labeled people may be going through similar life struggles and challenges. For example, they can be at various stages of developing their sexuality, exploring dating, and seeking to find or deepen an intimate relationship. Some are taking steps to become increasingly employable in the competitive world, while others are contemplating these options. Many are considering a move into a group home or unsupervised apartment or a move out of a parents' home.

Labeled people also have in common the problem of stigma. Ironically, they do not usually talk openly with each other about these problems. Studies have discovered their preoccupation with stigma but little if any evidence that they are assisting and supporting each other in coping with this problem (Dudley, 1983; Edgerton, 1993).

Numerous models for working with people in small groups have been developed by practice theorists in professions like social work and clinical psychology (e.g., Roberts & Northen, 1976). Among these practice models, the mediating model offers a useful approach in working with people who are confronting their oppressive conditions (Shulman, 1992). This model recognizes the group as a "system of mutual aid;" group members help each other, particularly in areas of common need.

Using the mediating model, a primary role of the group facilitator is to help each member and the group as a whole discover and develop their capacity for mutual aid. The tasks of the group facilitator include helping members share and discuss relevant information about themselves in the group, including helping them discuss taboo issues.

Groups are helpful in other ways as well. Individual members often find it easier to overcome their fears when functioning as part of a group. Other group members can encourage them to consider new ideas and skills, and to practice new behaviors using role plays and other simulation exercises.

A note of caution is needed about groups. Not everyone is well suited to a group. Some people may be too timid to participate in groups or may not be able to be attentive to the needs of others. In such instances, individual counseling is a likely alternative, or individual help could be offered to support participation in a group (Blotzer & Ruth, 1995).

Dispelling the Conspiracy of Silence

Most people find it difficult to talk with others about their disabilities and stigma problems. Obviously, these are not casual topics. In research studies, labeled people have revealed their experiences with stigma only after they have had long-term relationships with an outsider (Zetlin & Turner, 1984). A safe setting is needed that encourages self-disclosure without judgement and disrespect. Also, groups may need to go through phases, such as denial, recognition, exploration, and acceptance, to successfully self-disclose about these issues (Szivos & Griffiths, 1990).

A further obstacle to discussions of these topics needs to be addressed.

A taboo still exists in many settings about openly discussing a person's disability in his or her presence. Lorber (1974) identifies this as a "conspiracy of silence," which he describes as an unspoken agreement among helping people that the topic of their consumers' disabilities is not to be talked about in their presence. It is based on the misguided notion that such discussions serve no useful purpose or may be harmful because they encourage the person to dwell on a problem that cannot be overcome. Ironically, this notion tends to further peoples' beliefs that their disabilities are too undesirable to be mentioned, which only compounds the problem. Labeled people are also parties to the conspiracy of silence, as they have been taught that these discussions are counter-productive or an inappropriate intrusion into their privacy.

There are different ways of focusing on the topics of disabilities and stigma in peer groups. In many cases, these topics emerge while discussing other topics of interest, and the group facilitator can help the members focus on them. In other instances, these topics may need to be brought up by the facilitator if they are to be discussed at all. Examples of group sessions follow that illustrate these different ways of addressing peoples' disabilities and stigma issues.

A Group Focusing on Friendship and Dating

The most likely way to discuss stigma issues in a group is to respond to them as they come up while discussing other topics. A peer group that I have worked with provides an example. This group began as a discussion group on dating issues. The group members were labeled adults of different ages who were fairly independent. They lived in group homes, apartments, or with their parents. All of them could get to the sessions on their own by driving, using public transportation, or having someone else drive them. Most of them had prior knowledge of each other through other programs of the sponsoring agency. Sessions were always open to new members and attendance at sessions varied from 15 to 25 people.

The overall purpose of the group was identified by prospective group members, not by outsiders like staff or parents. Therefore, the members were ready to "work" soon after the initial ground rules were explained (e.g., confidentiality and respecting each other's views) and opportunities were provided for open discussion.

After structuring the first few sessions based on a well known training model, I discovered that this group was highly self-motivated and did not need such structure. I introduced the mediating model (described above) and began to "get out of the way" of the group's desire to do its private work. A new, more flexible structure evolved that was group-driven and could be used in other groups with similar purposes. This structure was based on several guidelines.

The first guideline was to make time available initially in each session for each person to briefly share something personal. This initial exercise was very helpful in involving people and giving them a chance to mention personal issues, problems, or accomplishments occurring since we last met. The exercise also helped members to become more aware of each other and to develop an agenda for each session.

In early sessions, most of the topics focused on dating and intimacy, the explicit purposes of the group. Examples of topics included, "How do I get noticed by a guy I like without scaring him away?" "How do I get my parents to let me date a guy?" "What should I do when a special friend interferes in my space?" "How do I meet new people?" and "What do I do with a new friend to get to know her better?"

A second guideline naturally followed: One or two topics were selected from the initial sharing time for more lengthy discussions. Active, high energy discussions usually erupted once a topic was chosen. A member would identify a concern and other members would provide helpful suggestions to that member. Sometimes other members shared similar concerns and suggestions were directed to them as well. For example, the topic: "How do I get noticed by a particular guy?" led to suggestions like "Be patient," "Express your need," and "Back off if he seems upset." Some of the more experienced members shared stories about what they did to win over their current partners. At times, role plays were introduced on these specific topics as well.

Another guideline was to close each session with each member having the opportunity to share any loose ends or closing comments about the session. During this brief time, some shared what they liked or learned from the session, what disappointed them, specific feelings that they had, and what they wanted to discuss next time. Sometimes we added a ritual of holding hands as we shared closing thoughts. Often we ended our sessions with a tentative decision about an agenda for the next session.

Another guideline was that group rules could be added or discarded as the group progressed. This allowed the group mem-

bers to freely establish ground rules that were needed to get their work done. Several rules were identified over time, such as only one person should talk at one time, everyone would get a chance to talk during the session, it was important to listen to others as well as talk, and members should raise their hands to be called on before talking when more than one person wanted to speak. All agreed that feelings were good to express and important to acknowledge and support. Modifications in these rules and additional rules were made as the group continued to meet.

This group, like most groups, had some excessive talkers and some very quiet ones. As the group facilitator, I helped both types of members adjust to the needs of the group as a whole. The talkers who tended to dominate were encouraged to listen more, and the group developed ground rules to help make this happen. Typically, the quieter members had little experience in social groups and benefited from just listening. Occasionally, they were encouraged to speak if they had something to say; their comments reminded the other members of their presence and helped them to gradually become more active.

Discussing Their Disabilities and Stigma

As the group continued to meet, the topics of the group expanded. While dating continued to be a major focus, other topics were added with some involving stigma issues. For example, one member wanted to explore the option of moving out of his parents' home into a group home. Another disliked being compared to a younger cousin who was "smarter"; he wanted advice on what to do. Another wanted to discuss what to do when other people did not like her or could not accept her disability. One member wanted to explore whether or not he could learn to drive after being told by a family member that it was not possible because he had Down syndrome?

Excerpts from a session on "being different and not accepted" offers an illustration of how a discussion about stigma can develop. This session occurred after the group had been meeting for several months. The topic was introduced during the previous session by Jake as, "What do I do when there is something about me that other people do not like?" (He is small and has Down syndrome.) This was the most open discussion about stigma up to that point.

Jake began by sharing something that he had never publicly disclosed to anyone before.

Jake:	"I want to talk about my being small. Some people ask me why I am so small ... What should I say?"
Don:	(spontaneously) "I'm small too. Children ask me the same question. I know that they don't know better."
Facilitator:	"This seems to be a very important topic for Jake and Don. Can we talk about it?" I encouraged others to share their thoughts and feelings.

Others immediately connected with this topic as they admitted to personal experiences in which they felt different and unaccepted.

Dara:	"My sister's boyfriend has trouble with me. I don't like him."
Joanna:	"I'm having trouble at work. They want me to do more on my job ... and they push me around. Why do they do this to me?"
Facilitator:	I asked them to explore these issues in more depth with the question, "Why do you think they do, Joanna?"
Peter:	(spontaneously) "Slow ... she's slow."

Others chimed in "slow" and "slower," revealing that they had had similar encounters at their work sites.

Mildred, modeling a way of addressing this problem said, "I have one eye blind. I'm slower because of it. I stay at my desk at lunch to complete my work because I know it won't be done on time. It will take me longer."

The session continued with others sharing their experiences and a few members like Mildred providing support and advice. As the facilitator, I expressed interest in all of their concerns. I occasionally gave advice and mostly encouraged them to share their experiences and solutions with each other.

Meetings like this one were very beneficial to members of the group. This session was one of the first times that many of them had ever talked with anyone about some of these topics, particularly the subject of stigma. As many shared their experiences, they began to feel more comfortable with themselves because their disabilities did not feel so burdensome. They also felt increasingly empowered by the discovery that they had much in common and were not alone.

While quick solutions were not readily evident, mutual aid was multiplying. Some of the more experienced members offered advice by drawing on their own experiences. Others with less experience also joined in with support and ideas. As these discussions strengthened their bonds with each other, their system of mutual aid expanded to include more frequent phone calls and get-togethers outside group meetings.

The group met monthly for two years. Over this time, the people in this group made an unusual amount of headway in their lives. After the group stopped meeting, all but a few members were involved in some type of male/female relationship. In contrast, few were dating before the group began. A couple in the group was planning to get married, and one member was about to move from his family's home to more independent living. Several of them had improved their work situations after becoming more open and assertive about their needs.

Groups Designed to Discuss Stigma Problems

Stigma problems can be extremely painful and debilitating to labeled people. These problems become compounded when someone does not know what to do and has nowhere to turn for help. In such cases, peer groups can be established to help people understand and confront these problems. Many relevant topics on stigma can be discussed. Promoting self-understanding can be a place to begin.

Promoting Self-Understanding

Who Am I? Labeled people, like all of us, should have a good sense of who they are and feel good about themselves. Some general questions can be explored in groups that help members consider this topic. As group members reflect upon how they think and feel about themselves, their strengths and limitations are likely to be identified. Stigma issues are also likely to emerge. Topics for groups wanting to work on self-concept issues could consider any of the following questions (McLennan, 1984):

- What do I think about myself?
- What parts of me do I like?
- In what situations do I feel good about myself?
- What parts of me do I not like?
- In what situations don't I feel good about myself?
- How do others feel about me?
  - My family
  - My friends
  - Staff members
  - People where I work
- How could I feel better about myself?

What Is My Disability? As groups discuss self-concept issues, the topic of a person's disability is important to explore (Blotzer & Ruth, 1995). A disability is an important aspect of one's identity which may impose physical, intellectual, or social challenges to normal functioning.

If labeled people want to understand their disability, they may need to have individualized medical information about it, including the etiology (if known) and professional judgement about the challenges that it may impose and the extent to which these challenges can be overcome. As I mentioned initially, mental retardation is not a monolithic medical condition but a label that comprises over 250 known physiological and mental conditions and many more conditions with unknown causes.

Generally, when people labeled with mental retardation have described their disabilities in research studies, they have shared accurate information. However, they tend to emphasize the physical aspects or a specific learning deficiency while denying a general mental disability (Dudley, 1983; Turner, Kernan, & Gelphman, 1984; Zetlin & Turner, 1984). These omissions may be deliberate because many labeled people perceive a greater degree of stigma to be associated with a general mental disability or mental retardation.

Do I Have Mental Retardation? Another important topic to explore in peer groups is the mental retardation label and related issues. The controversy that surrounds this label becomes evident when labeled people are asked the question of whether they perceive themselves as having mental retardation. Studies indicate that a fairly large percentage of the people who are known by this label are privy to the controversies about labels in general and the mental retardation label in particular (e.g., Dudley, 1983; Edgerton, 1993).

Some questions that could be explored in peer group discussions about the mental retardation label include the following:

1. What do people mean by mental retardation?
2. Mental retardation is a label. What does that mean?
3. How does one become labeled mentally retarded? What's bad about it? Are there any advantages to being labeled?
4. Do I have a mental retardation label?
5. How was this determined?
6. Who are the people who say I am labeled with mental retardation?
7. Are there people who do not perceive me in this way?

8. How can people tell that I have this label? How do they show that they know?
9. Will I always have this label?
10. Can I do anything to remove the label?

Group Illustrations

One group that focused on labeling issues illustrates how a group can begin discussing this topic (McLennan, 1984). The purposes of this group session were to help the three members to have more understanding of the mental retardation label and its effect on them. The group discussed this topic after meeting several times. Some of the questions identified above under "Do I have mental retardation?" were used to focus the discussion.

After initial "small talk" to get the session started, the group facilitator focused on the topic of the day.

> *Facilitator:* "We have been dealing with personal concerns a lot lately. Last week we talked about what makes us feel good about ourselves and what makes us feel bad about ourselves. Today I would like to talk about mental retardation. What do people mean by 'mental retardation?'"

All three women look at the facilitator very seriously and attentively. No one offered a response.

> *Facilitator:* "Does anyone have any ideas about what people mean by mental retardation?"
>
> *Rita:* "Ah . . . the elderly."
>
> *Facilitator:* "You think old people are labeled mentally retarded?"
>
> *Rita:* "Yes. My grandmother is very old. She is deaf and blind."
>
> *Facilitator:* "Does anyone have anything to say about what Rita has just said?"

Martha is looking at me very intently.

> *Facilitator:* "I see wheels turning in your head, Martha, what are you thinking?"

Martha smiles and is quiet for several seconds.

> *Martha:* "I don't know."
>
> *Facilitator:* "This is a touchy question. People don't talk about this very often. It is hard to know how we feel about something that we never talk about or even think about too

much . . . but it *is* important to take our time and think about this."

Silence occurs for a short time.

Facilitator: "Let's ask ourselves, 'What do people mean by mental retardation?' "

Kristin: "When people walk funny."

Facilitator: "OK, Kristin, what else do you think people mean by mental retardation?"

Kristin: "When people talk funny."

Rita: "When you are born. Like if you were born brain damaged."

Facilitator: "How about if we deal with some personal questions. Let's all ask ourselves the question, 'Am I mentally retarded?' "

Rita: "No. I have problems with my back. When I was little I was playing and I fell and my retarded cousin kicked me in the back and I have scoliosis in my back. I was twelve."

Facilitator: "Does your back cause you pain now?"

Rita: "No. Sometimes."

Facilitator looks at Martha.

Martha: "I used to be retarded. That's why they put me in (institution)."

Rita: "I'm part retarded."

Facilitator: "So you think you're part retarded, Rita?"

Rita: "Yes" and nods her head.

Facilitator: "Martha, you think that's why you were put in (institution)?"

Martha: "I was retarded. My parents didn't think I could get along in school, so they put me in (institution)."

Facilitator: "Kristin, you're usually very talkative. You've been very quiet. How do you feel . . . what do *you* think about the question, 'Am I mentally retarded?' "

Kristin nods slowly and says: "Yes. I am."

Facilitator: "Why Kristin?"

Kristin: "Because I talk funny."

Facilitator:	"You think because you have a hard time talking some-times, that you are mentally retarded?"
Kristin:	"Yes, and I walk funny too."
Facilitator:	"How was this decided? How was this decided that you are mentally retarded?"
Martha:	"The doctor decided. He decided I was."
Rita:	"Yes, the doctor. Like if you are born with brain damage. I was, I think, and the doctor told my parents. You can check my records. It's in my records about my brain damage."
Facilitator:	"Kristin, who decides a person is mentally retarded."
Kristin:	"The doctor . . . and sometimes at school. The teacher."
Facilitator:	"Do you think teachers decide if a person should be called mentally retarded or not?"
Kristin:	"Sometimes."

In retrospect, the group facilitator noted that she talked too much, tried to cover too many issues, and did not encourage enough interchange among the members. However, she also noted that the members were not as talkative as usual because of the nature of the questions being asked. Other facilitators may also find that groups are more inhibited as they begin to discuss disability and stigma topics, suggesting the need for the facilitator to take a more active role for awhile.

As labeled people gain a better understanding of their disabilities and labels, they can more fully comprehend the stigma in their lives. Because people with a mental retardation label are encountering stigma in their everyday lives, they need a place to bring these concerns for exploration, examination, and problem solving. Peer group discussion can provide an outlet for expressing pent-up feelings of anguish, fear, frustration, anger, and powerlessness.

Help is also needed in understanding particular stigma encounters. Specifically this help may include distinguishing stigma problems from disability-related ones, discerning the origins of problems and the specific motives of the stigma promoters, and analyzing the part played by the labeled person in encouraging or discouraging these encounters.

Chapter 6 describes several ways that labeled people have learned to cope with and manage stigma problems. Four different coping strategies are highlighted beyond initial attempts to learn how to cope. These strategies include seeking the positive aspects of being labeled, confronting stigma, passing, and covering. These patterns and others should be viewed as options that can be taken by people labeled with mental retardation in their attempts to manage stigma.

All reasonable strategies or options for managing and overcoming stigma can be explored in peer group sessions. As members share their own experiences, strategies can be offered by more experienced group members, and role play situations can be introduced to rehearse ways of handling a stigma encounter. Experimentation with these strategies between group sessions can also be encouraged, providing material for discussions in subsequent sessions.

The group of three women described above began talking about stigma encounters in a later session. Excerpts from this sessions follow.

Rita:	"Sometimes people stare at me and they call me that (mentally retarded)."
Facilitator:	"Who does that, Rachel?"
Rita:	"My cousins sometimes."
Facilitator:	"How does that make you feel?"
Rita:	"Very bad . . . "
Facilitator:	"You brought up a very important concern, Rita. Has anyone else had someone stare at them or tease them?"
Kristin:	"Hmm, hmm. Yeah sometimes . . . Sometimes they are looking at my walking or when I talk."
Facilitator:	"How do you feel, Kristin?"
Kristin:	"Not good. I don't like it."
Facilitator:	"I can really understand why, Kristin. I know when I have been teased, I have felt like I was different and I didn't belong. Does anyone feel like that—like you want to hide or something?"
Kristin:	"Yeah . . . "
Facilitator:	"What is a good way to handle staring?"
Kristin:	"Ignore them."
Rita:	"Yeah, ignore them. That's what I do."
Facilitator:	"Yes. Does that work?"
Kristin:	"Yes."
Martha:	"I tell them to cut it out . . . to stop staring . . . what are they looking at anyway . . . "

This discussion continued awhile longer about their various encounters with staring, a topic that seemed new to the conversations of these three women.

Private work, like the illustrations above, can open up new horizons to labeled people. After gaining new insights into their individual identities and social circumstances, some may want to join the self-advocacy movement. They may also want to advocate for their rights within the mental retardation settings where they receive services. Others may want to explore options for delabeling and disengaging from the mental retardation system. The next three chapters explore these options.

References

Blotzer, M., & Ruth, R. (1995). *Sometimes you just want to feel like a human being: Case studies of empowering psychotherapy with people with disabilities.* Baltimore: Paul H. Brookes.

Coleman, L. (1986). Stigma: An enigma demystified. In S. Ainlay, G. Becker, & L. Coleman (Eds.), *The dilemma of difference: A multidisciplinary view of stigma,* pp. 211–232. New York: Plenum.

Dudley, J. (1983). *Living with stigma: The plight of the people who we label mentally retarded.* Springfield, IL: Charles C Thomas.

Edgerton, R. (1993). *Cloak of competence: Stigma in the lives of the mentally retarded.* (Revised and Updated Edition). Los Angeles: University of California Press.

Edwards, J. (1982). *We are people first: Our handicaps are secondary.* Portland: Ednick.

Gibbons, F. (1986). Stigma and interpersonal relations. In S. Ainlay, G. Becker, & L. Coleman (Eds.), *The dilemma of difference: A multidisciplinary view of stigma,* pp. 123–144. New York: Plenum.

Lorber, M. (1974). Consulting the mentally retarded: An approach to the definition of mental retardation by experts. Unpublished doctoral dissertation, University of California at Los Angeles.

McLennan, H. (1984). Process record of a group discussion on the label of mental retardation, Unpublished paper.

Roberts, R., & Northen, H. (1976). *Theories of social work with groups.* New York: Columbia University Press.

Shulman, L. (1992). *The skills of helping: Individuals, families, and groups,* 3rd ed. Itasca, Illinois: F.E. Peacock Publishers.

Szivos, S., & Griffiths, E. (1990). Group processes involved in coming to terms with a mentally retarded identity. *Mental Retardation,* 28(6), 333–341.

Turner, J., Kernan, K., & Gelphman, S. (1984). Speech etiquette in a sheltered workshop. In R. Edgerton (Ed.), *Lives in process: Mildly retarded adults in a large city* pp. 43–71. Washington, D.C.: American Association on Mental Retardation.

Williams, P., & Shoultz, B. (1982). *We can speak for ourselves: Self-advocacy by mentally handicapped people.* Bloomington: Indiana University press.

Zetlin, A., & Turner, J. (1984). Self-perspectives on being handicapped: Stigma and adjustment. In R. Edgerton (Ed.), *Lives in process: Mildly retarded adults in a large city* pp. 93–120. Washington, D.C.: American Association on Mental Retardation.

Chapter 10

ADVOCATING FOR SELF–ADVOCACY

*. . . I would say, **Listen,** is one of the key words for (nondisabled people), and **Speak For Yourself** is the key word for people with disabilities (People First of Washington, 1985, p. 11).*

To me, self-advocacy means helping other handicapped people learn what you have learned. It means to help them accomplish more than they ever dreamed of accomplishing. It helped me to grow and handle my handicap as though it was nothing to be afraid of or worry about. I've been able to live as though I don't have a handicap at all (Williams & Shoultz, 1982, p. 86).

Self-advocacy means . . . speaking about your own rights. The right to education, the right to vote, the right to work, and the right to live independently. Another important right . . . (to) go to the mall without worrying about people looking at us funny as a person with a disability. We are human beings and not just a person with a disability (Nichols, 1996).

People who are labeled with mental retardation may be one of the last oppressed groups in our society to collectively organize, following after a distinguished list of self-advocacy groups like the civil rights movement, the women's movement, and the Gray Panthers.

Like these other disenfranchised groups, people labeled with mental retardation are coming to realize that they will not succeed without speaking for themselves. Many of them have concluded that they can be more effective as self-advocates than relying on others to advocate for them.

People with disabilities may be the best people to speak in neighborhood meetings when someone asks why they should live there. They may be the best educators of company executives and middle managers about the benefits of hiring people with disabilities. They may be the most powerful lobbyists advocating for adequate funding for their programs. They may have the greatest influence with agency administrators of the System in promoting supported employment, greater independence, and societal inclusion for consumers. In short, they may be the best advocates for themselves and other labeled people.

A self-advocacy movement has emerged in the United States and in other parts of the world. Its beginnings can be traced back to Sweden in 1967 when a group of people with disabilities informed their local parent advocacy group that they wanted to start speaking for themselves. By 1974, the movement spread to this country, first appearing as the "People First Movement" in Salem, Oregon.

What Is Self-Advocacy?

What is self-advocacy? A recent **definition of self-advocacy** adopted by leaders of the national self-advocacy organization is:

> Self-advocacy is teaching people with a disability how to advocate for themselves and to learn how to speak out for what they believe in. It teaches us how to make decisions and choices that affect our lives so we can become more independent. It also teaches us about our rights, but along with learning our rights, we learn our responsibilities. (Hayden & Shoultz, 1991, p. 4)

The next three scenes illustrate what is happening in this movement.

Scene 1: A convention is taking place at the Sheraton Hotel. People are sitting at several round tables that span a large meeting room. Some seem bewildered, others are idly looking at materials that have been handed out, and still others are excitedly caucusing with each other. A speaker emerges at the front of the room and begins to speak. He shares his early childhood memories of how a doctor told his mother he would never be able to walk and thereafter how he struggled to become mobile. His closing remarks are these:

> We can go as far as you allow us to go. We can go as far as we allow ourselves to go. So if we work together who knows how far hand in hand we can travel together? We need and want jobs to provide for ourselves and also for our personal pride. Just because we don't walk straight on the outside does not mean we cannot stand tall on the inside.

Scene 2: A leader of another self-advocacy group 800 miles to the north of the first scene exhorts to the hundreds gathering together, "You have to make thunder. You have to speak for your rights. You're not going to get in no trouble speaking for yourself, because there aren't going to be laws in this room. I want to hear thunder! (Shapiro, 1991)."

Scene 3: Three thousand miles to the west, Judy Curio, a former resident of a state institution, delivered the keynote address to her self-advocacy convention. Excerpts included, "Being free is being accepted by society for what you are; to be free to live the way you want to and not be put down for something that is out of your control. Get to know a beautiful person inside a deformed body." The audience erupted with a resounding round of applause (Edwards, 1982, p. 21).

These are illustrations drawn from three of more than 700 self-advocacy groups known to exist in 48 states (Hayden, Lakin, & Braddock, & Smith, 1995). The number of organizations and participants in this movement has exploded during the past few years and have established a critical mass of self-advocates. Thousands more are participating in other parts of the world as well (Dybwad & Bersani, 1996).

What Do Self-Advocacy Groups Do?

Societal myths have undoubtedly delayed this movement's emergence. At one time, we thought that labeled people needed others to speak for them. Now we know that they are capable of having their own collective voice. At one time they were thought to be lacking in the skills needed to organize and implement self-advocacy. Over time they have proven this to be untrue. Their views were once considered unimportant, but now we know that they have very important things to say to us.

Over the past several years, this movement has undertaken an enormously ambitious agenda and has accomplished an impressive set of achievements that were previously considered unthinkable. The number of people currently involved in the movement is an impressive achievement in itself. Local self-advocacy groups have recruited thousands of labeled people and helped them with support and encouragement, training, tangible assistance, and individual advocacy (Dybwad & Bersani, 1996; Longhurst, 1994; Williams & Shoultz, 1982).

Self-advocacy groups have been involved in letter writing to public officials, service providers, and others. They have arranged and run countless meetings of local groups, and they have coordinated complex regional and state conventions as well. They have established numerous organizational newsletters that reveal who they are and what they believe. They have assisted service providers with fact finding projects, evaluations of service provisions, and educational forums on pertinent topics.

Self-advocates have not usually been known to be militant, for example, to participate in adversarial activities like demonstrations, boycotts, and legal actions. But they have taken on some courageous challenges. Some groups have advocated for closing institutions and others have protested cutbacks to community services (Longhurst, 1994). The national organization is currently pursuing some bold concerns as well, including changing guardianship laws, seeking fair wages in employment, and seeking changes in Medicaid and Supplemental Security Income programs.

The achievements of a regional group in the Philadelphia area further illustrate the power of this movement. According to one of their annual reports, their accomplishments have been impressive (Speaking for Ourselves, 1987). For example, their members gave a formal presentation to a public law center on closing a nearby institution. Officers were interviewed on a popular radio station and by the local newspaper about their work. One member testified before a United States Senate committee on Medicaid reform, while others gave a presentation to a statewide convention of employees of the mental health and mental retardation system. And to top off this list, several members conducted a statewide interview study of other consumers about their satisfaction with their employment.

Besides being involved in self-advocacy efforts, these groups also devote an enormous amount of time developing and sustaining their memberships. Often, a self-advocacy organization has a steering or coordinating committee and several smaller support groups (Williams & Shoultz, 1982). The steering committee helps to initiate participation in support groups, plans coordinated efforts, and sponsors annual conventions. The support groups recruit new people, teach them about self-advocacy, develop their skills in running meetings, and assist individual members having problems. Training their members and sponsoring conventions, two of their tasks, are examined more closely below.

Training

Training members to become effective self-advocates is an important part of the self-advocacy movement. An illustration of a training session of one group follows (Smith, 1985). Instructions for leading this session are presented in a methodical way that can be easily followed by a new leader. Important concepts are reviewed and a step-by-step guide is offered for easy implementation. Focused discussions and exercises are emphasized.

The session begins with minutes of the last meeting being read and approved (Smith, 1985). Someone is assigned to record the minutes for this meeting. The agenda for today's session is introduced. The members are asked what the word, "agenda" means, for review.

Today's agenda is "communicating problems." The leader is instructed to begin with:

"Today we are going to talk about the problems that we have. What is a problem?" If they are having difficulty with the answer, ask the group to recall when they were mad at someone in the group home (or work, etc.) last. Ask them to describe why they were mad . . . Emphasize that problems make us mad. Because we are mad, we would like to change or fix the problem.

(Next) say "Now let's start to discuss some of our problems that each of us might have. I'll start." The instructor will begin by expressing a problem or concern that he or she has in daily life. . . . A good concern might be the problem of getting one's roommate/spouse to do their share of the chores.

The next steps in communicating problems are reviewed. For example, as people take turns sharing their problems, the leader's role is to ask for clarity. For example, the leader might ask, "repeat the problem," "ask for an example," "determine if it is a problem for others by asking them to raise their hands." Throughout the discussion, the leader is encouraged to give positive reinforcement for problem statements that sound clear and legitimate.

Conventions

Conventions are an important part of the self-advocacy movement just as they are for professional groups. Many labeled people look forward to the annual conventions long before they are held. Different types of events occur at these conventions, including keynote addresses by prominent guest speakers, plenary sessions, concurrent workshops, displays of vendors, and time for socializing and networking.

The 1994 National Self-Advocacy Convention provides an example of the happenings of one convention (Cone, 1994). Many lively speakers and presentations addressed various topics like moving from institutions to the community, closing institutions, building strong self-advocacy groups, and the rights of individuals in the criminal justice system.

A sense of fellowship and community emerged among the participants at this national convention. As experiences were shared, common needs were discovered. Emotions were particularly strong at the workshops as presenters drew on their life experiences. Their memories were in many ways negative, such as recalling physical abuse, segregation, loss of familial contact, loss of decision-making opportunities, and deterioration of abilities and skills due to idleness (Cone, 1994).

Two issues were raised many times: freedom and fear. Freedom was talked about in relation to institutional placements, and the necessity of having choice in work, living arrangement, friends, making decisions, and making mistakes. Fears were expressed about not having enough freedom, and fear that freedom would be denied by others, particularly staff members and parents.

While local self-advocacy conventions are similar to the national convention described above, differences are evident as well. Local conventions include participants ranging from the seasoned leaders to beginners and curious first timers. The types of workshop topics are different as well, addressing issues more at the personal than political level, such as: "how to protect yourself," "the Americans with Disabilities Act and how it works for you," "how to say 'no' when you do not want to be touched," "safe sex and AIDS," "how to meet new people to date," "interviewing for a job," and "addressing employment problems."

Preparation for Conventions

Ad hoc groups can be formed to help people prepare for their self-advocacy convention. I have helped to set up several such groups with university students assigned as facilitators. These groups are usually composed of people who are not members of a self-advocacy group but are interested in attending a convention. These ad hoc groups usually meet weekly for six to eight times prior to the state convention. The groups are small, usually less than 10 people. They are often people residing in the same group home or living within close geographic proximity of each other.

The facilitators introduce several concepts to these groups. The concept of self-advocacy is the primary one. Other important concepts are power, empowerment, rights, assertiveness, and self-esteem. The group sessions are relaxed and informal.

After these ad hoc groups have discussed the purposes of self-advocacy and its relevance to them, the convention agenda is usually introduced and the different types of activities are described, such as plenary sessions, keynote speakers, and the workshops.

The specific workshop topics of the convention are introduced and members are encouraged to select one or two topics of interest. Time is then spent talking about these topics and exploring personal questions and issues that the members may want to raise at such a workshop. An example is a workshop topic on the Americans with Disabilities Act. The basic concept of civil rights can be discussed, with a focus on specific rights reflected in some of the sections of the law, for example, employment, transportation, and public accommodations. These brief presentations can be interspersed with discussions about the members' problems or rights in these areas.

These ad hoc groups accomplish many objectives. They offer a brief introduction to self-advocacy. Discussions about topics evolve to become preconvention deliberations that can be continued at the convention. Members also have an opportunity to prepare themselves for the convention by obtaining new information and ideas, practicing new speaking skills, and feeling greater self-confidence.

Usually, these ad hoc groups have a final session after the convention is over for a debriefing. Members share their experiences from the convention, what they have learned, their excitement, and their disappointments. The ad hoc group's ending is also discussed in this last session, and members are encouraged to take the next step—becoming active with their local self-advocacy group.

Stages of Self-Advocacy Groups

An advisor of one "People First" chapter has conceptualized three stages that self-advocacy groups tend to go through as they move toward greater independence (Curtis, 1984). These stages are not an exact fit for every group, but they offer a set of benchmarks for groups to consider in evaluating how far along they have progressed toward independence.

The first stage is the **"beginning"** or formative period for a chapter. This stage may last for several years. Officers are elected and learn their duties. Members are taught to prepare their agendas, to conduct meetings, and to make decisions. A constitution or bylaws can be written. Membership drives and other means of recruitment are instituted.

The second stage is called **"learning to be independent."** By now, the chapter has several experienced members. With assistance, they are able to set up and conduct meetings, and recruit new members. Some of the members have developed self-advocacy skills. For example, they can write letters to legislators and others, draw up and circulate petitions, and speak to the media.

The third stage is a point in time when a chapter has obtained **considerable independence.** Members can do all of the things that they did in the previous stage without assistance, including conducting meetings, having experienced leaders, and recruiting new members.

The leaders are intimately familiar with their legal rights by now, and their advocacy skills have become refined and increasingly effective.

By the third stage, members are ready to share more of their expertise with the larger community. They may conduct training sessions for staff members and other self-advocacy groups. Some members are ready to serve on the boards of mental retardation agencies and organizations like the local ARC. Some members are increasingly called on to speak at professional conventions and at the self-advocacy conventions of other groups. At this stage the chapter may closely resemble the self-advocacy groups of people with physical disabilities (Curtis, 1984).

Members will want to periodically evaluate their group's development and whether it has moved from one stage to the next. One way to do this is to help the group to identify its strengths and accomplishments as a group and as individual members. They may also reflect on how they do things in comparison to the past; for example, are they running meetings more proficiently than they did at an earlier time in the chapter's life.

It should be noted that many groups may never reach the third stage. Most groups may stay at the second stage and some may not easily get beyond stage one. In one locality, for example, after several years of functioning, only one of seven chapters reached stage three, some were fixed at the second stage, and the remaining ones were still working in the beginning stage (Curtis, 1984).

The Supporter's Role

Self-advocacy groups are assisted by a person with or without a disability who works closely with them. This person has been called an "advisor," "supporter," and "coordinator." While "advisor" has been the most familiar term used, some feel that "advisor" conveys too much control and not enough emphasis on being an assistant to a group and equal in status (Lazzara, 1996). "Supporter" is used in this book because it conveys less formality and is more descriptive of what the person does.

Supporters to self-advocacy groups need to have special qualities to be effective (Curtis, 1984; ILSMH, 1996). These qualities are similar to the qualities generally required of an "ally," described in Chapter 7. Effective supporters are interested in the welfare of labeled people and have respect for them as individuals. They have understanding of the special needs of people with disabilities. They are personable and open-minded, available when needed, and committed to the self-advocacy movement.

They also can work well with small groups. Most important, they are able to be continually sensitive to the balance needed in doing enough to assist but not doing what group members can do for themselves.

Self-advocacy groups should play an active role in selecting who their "supporters" will be. People First of Washington (1985) suggest that groups should recruit and interview prospective supporters and select their preferences. They can make up a contract with the supporter that states what the person in this role is supposed to do. Other suggestions include training the supporter about the group's needs, and creating a committee of the group to periodically meet with and evaluate the supporter. Supporters should support such efforts as well because they reflect an important aspect of what self-advocacy is about — having control over your own life.

Preparation for Becoming a Supporter

Often prospective supporters realize that they have personal work to do to prepare themselves for this work. Two personal-related tasks may need to be worked on.

Task 1: Coming to Terms with Personal Biases: Prospective supporters may have misconceptions about people who are labeled with mental retardation that can interfere with their efforts to help. They may, for example, believe that labeled people do not have the ability to be self-advocates. This judgement may be based on an awareness that some labeled people do not yet manifest strong abilities in advocacy. In fact, many new recruits to this movement are likely to present themselves as immature, shy, helpless, or bewildered. This is likely the result of their previous socialization that has not nurtured the self-confidence and skills needed by self-advocates.

Prospective supporters may also have internalized other societal myths that could interfere with the helping role of a supporter. For example, they may be overly concerned about the risks that labeled people will be taking as they embark on new unchartered territory. Motivated by these feelings, they may view themselves more as "protectors" who discourage risk-taking than supporters who encourage it. Such supporters may have to question whether their motives to help are based on sympathy and guilt rather than empathy, confidence, and hopefulness.

Task 2: Redefining Old Roles: Human service personnel who work in the mental retardation system are among the most likely to volunteer to be supporters. Ironically, they may be more affected by some societal myths than other people, as they are likely to have internalized various consumer stereotypes that have been perpetrated by the System where they work. For example, consumers in the mental retardation system have the role of "recipient" of service, they are expected to be dependent on their service providers, and they are seldom viewed as experts or serious participants in decisions affecting their lives.

In addition, human service workers who want to become supporters could easily find that their helping roles in the System are, by definition, in conflict with the expectations of a supporter (Curtis, 1984; ILSMH, 1996; Williams & Shoultz, 1982). This problem could become apparent, for example, if a manager of a adult training center acts as a supporter to a self-advocacy group that includes trainees from the same center. This supporter will have obvious limitations in encouraging the self-advocates to raise concerns and protests about their training center or even other training facilities. Other problems can arise from the potential conflicts of interest of a supporter. The group members may be affected by their awareness of the supporter's employment role. For example, they may be hesitant in their actions because of a concern that it threatens their supporter's job.

Human service workers employed with the mental retardation field may have more personal work to do in preparing themselves than others; conversely, employees from other human service fields and other citizens may be better suited to assist in this movement. The latter groups will likely have less exposure to the stereotypes perpetrated by the delivery system serving these consumers.

Generally, the roles that all human service workers are trained to perform as practitioners need to be redefined if they are to be effective as self-advocacy supporters or allies. The roles that carry authority and decision-making responsibilities, for example, should not be acted upon.

Supporters should not consider themselves indispensable. Rather, they are often called to stand on the sidelines, watching the members run their own meetings and assisting them only when they need help. The process becomes more important to the supporter than the content of what is worked on, and the process must move at the members' pace.

According to one seasoned supporter, it can be very difficult for supporters to hold back their own ideas or goals when assisting a self-advocacy group (Lazzara, 1996). This supporter claims that listening to the group is most important. If he wants to say something, he often asks, "Is it ok if I talk?" before entering the discussion. When he shares his ideas, he is often helping the members consider whether or not what they are discussing relates to *their* intended goals. He almost always avoids answering a group's questions, and instead redirects the question back to them.

People First of Washington (1985, p. 20) provides supporters with questions that they should ask themselves periodically to determine their effectiveness and to avoid burnout. This group also has strong views about what supporters or advisors should do, such as:

- Advisors should help us when we need it. Help a little but not too much.
- Advisors should let us talk and run the meetings.
- Advisors should try to understand how consumers feel.
- Advisors should support our self-esteem, and care about us at all times.
- Advisors should help us overcome the fear of speaking to the public.
- Advisors should be someone who will talk ideas through with us.
- Advisors should believe in our movement.

Supporters' Roles at Different Stages

Supporters assist members with a broad array of tasks (Edwards, 1982; Williams & Shoultz, 1982). They help members to learn how to work as a group and to make their own decisions. They help in teaching advocacy skills, training officers for their respective positions, and assisting with public relations.

As pointed out above, self-advocacy groups can go through several stages toward greater independence. The role of supporters will vary depending upon the stage of a group. Supporters become less important and more ad hoc as a group becomes more independent in its functioning. A supporter to one People First chapter describes the changes in this role as a group becomes more independent (Curtis, 1994).

Beginning Stage: During the beginning stage, the supporter is often the dynamic force behind much of what is done. The supporter might introduce labeled people to the movement, educate them about its goals, and teach them how to start a chapter. After a chapter forms, supporters help officers learn their duties. They help set up meetings, working closely with the executive committee on the agenda. They teach rules of order, including staying on task and seeking participation from every member. They help teach the members advocacy skills, with the emphasis at this stage being on assertiveness training.

During this first stage of a group, staff members of mental retardation agencies are often the most likely people to be supporters because they are accessible and more acutely aware of the need for this movement than outsiders. Nevertheless, other volunteers can also be effective supporters in this beginning stage.

Learning to Become Independent Stage: During the "learning to be independent" stage, the supporter's role becomes less central. Supporters attend executive and chapter meetings and assist when needed. The supporters work with the more experienced members to help them teach new members about self-advocacy and running meetings. They help members learn how to make good decisions by problem-solving about their daily challenges. For example, members are helped to problem solve about how to manage disagreements among group home residents, or how to resolve conflicts with parents, counselors, or other employees. During this stage, supporters may be selected from a broader cross-section of the community, for example, interested community members, school teachers, university students, or friends of members, as well as human service workers.

Independence Stage: Once a group reaches the "independence" stage, the supporter may be a more experienced "People First" member from the chapter or a nearby chapter. The supporter at this stage is largely a consultant who offers advice, support, and other assistance to the leadership of the group when it is needed.

Ad hoc supporters may also be recruited to assist with focused needs. For example, a credit officer from a department store may provide assistance with purchasing goods on credit, a social studies teacher may educate them about the election process, and a lawyer may help with understanding human and civil rights. A teacher may help with writing letters to legislators or stories for the chapter's newsletter.

A Proposed Role for the Mental Retardation System
(Dudley, 1996)

The mental retardation system can be a more active player in supporting the self-advocacy movement. The System and its agencies have direct access to numerous consumers who could be recruited. Furthermore, they probably have the greatest influence over the lives of most consumers. I have several suggestions in this regard:

1. **Share Information:** Regularly inform your consumers about self-advocacy and the activities of the local self-advocacy organization. The concept of self-advocacy is not simple or easy to comprehend so time needs to be given to illuminating what it is. Also, the schedule for meetings, topics of meetings,

information about the state and regional conventions, and accomplishments of the movement should be periodically shared. An easily accessible bulletin board could be set aside just for self-advocacy information. Interest in this movement among consumer groups is usually directly related to how much they know about self-advocacy and how enthusiastic their agency personnel are about it.

2. Encourage Participation: Consumers will likely not be able to attend self-advocacy meetings without help. They may need regular assistance with transportation to meetings. They also may need help planning their schedules so that other activities do not compete with these meetings. Some consumers may want to become officers and may need encouragement and support to pursue these ambitions.

3. Help Establish a Local Self-Advocacy Group: If a self-advocacy group does not exist nearby your agency, help consumers establish one. There is considerable literature available on starting these groups (e.g., Cone, 1994; Curtis, 1984; Edwards, 1982; Hayden & Shoultz, 1991; People First of Washington, 1985; Williams & Shoultz, 1982). Officers of other self-advocacy groups can also help in starting up new groups. One important caveat for agencies assisting in forming a self-advocacy group is that the group must always be viewed as being independent of an agency and its agenda. Agencies must not attempt to use the group for their own purposes.

4. Convention Participation: Perhaps the self-advocacy conventions are the most exciting events of the movement. Encouraging interested consumers to attend local and state self-advocacy conventions are helpful. People who are interested in learning more about the movement will likely be inspired by attending such a convention. Specific support can be provided in several different ways. Newcomers will need help in understanding the purposes and events of conventions. Experienced self-advocates can be invited to speak to your consumers about the convention. The programs from previous conventions, particularly the lists of various workshops, could be shared. Also interested consumers will likely need transportation to the convention, and help with the costs of registration, meals, and a hotel if the convention is some distance away.

5. Encourage Staff Involvement: Encourage staff members to volunteer to help the movement if they are interested. These staff can assist the agency's consumers at the convention and volunteer to assist with workshops and other convention activities. Agencies can support their staff in these roles by considering their volunteer time as paid work for the agency. Some staff may also want to invest in self-advocacy beyond assisting at a convention. They may want to consider becoming supporters to local groups.

6. Listen to Their Voices: Listen to the voices of your consumers after they return from a convention or other self-advocacy meetings. Groups sessions could be formed among those who attended for processing what happened, discussing what was and was not helpful, and determining what participants may want to do next in relation to self-advocacy. Also, consumers who attended the convention should be given an opportunity to share their experiences with others who did not attend.

7. Listen to the Voices of the Movement: Many suggestions are offered by self-advocacy groups. Often these suggestions are directed to agencies serving labeled people; yet, administrators and staff members do not often consider these ideas as relevant to their service operations. Service providers are encouraged to periodically review and consider convention proceedings, newsletters, and informal comments of self-advocates as another set of standards for evaluating how well their programs are functioning.

References

Cone, A. (1994). Reflections on self-advocacy: Voices for choices. *Mental Retardation,* 32, (6), 444–445.

Curtis, C. (1984). The changing role of the people first advisor. *American Rehabilitation,* Spring, 1984, 6–9.

Dudley, J. (1996). Seeking a closer partnership with the self-advocacy movement. *Mental Retardation,* 34, (4), 255–256.

Dybwad, G., & Bersani, H. (Eds.) (1996). *New voices: Self-advocacy by people with disabilities.* Cambridge, MA: Brookline Books.

Edwards, J. (1982). We are people first: Our handicaps are secondary. Portland: Ednick.

Hayden, M., Lakin, C., Braddock, D., & Smith, G. (1995). Trends and milestones: Growth in self-advocacy organizations. *Mental Retardation,* 33, (5), 342.

Hayden, M., & Shoultz, B. (1991). *Self-advocacy by persons with disabilities — Ideas for creating a national organization.* Minneapolis: Institute on Community Integration (UAP), University of Minnesota.

ILSMH (International League of Societies for Persons with Mental Handicaps). (1996). *The beliefs, values, and principles of self-advocacy.* Cambridge, MA: Brookline Books.

Lazzara, N. (1996). Conversations with Neil R. Lazzara, who has worked for self-advocates for 20 years and currently works at the Massachusetts Department of Mental Retardation, 1537 Main Street, Springfield, MA, January, 1996.

Longhurst, N. (1994). *The self-advocacy movement by people with developmental disabilities: A demographic study and directory of self-advocacy groups in the United States.* Washington, D.C.: American Association on Mental Retardation.

Nichols, K. (1996). Community advocacy press: People with developmental disabilities speak out for what they believe, Vol. 1(1), p. 1. Cincinnati: Capabilities Unlimited, Inc. (a self-advocacy newsletter).

People First of Washington. (1985). *Speaking up and speaking out: An international self-advocacy movement.* Tacoma, WA: Report of the International Self-Advocacy Leadership Conference, July, 1984.

Shapiro, J. (1991). Pity is a four-letter word, *Fellowship Magazine,* September, 1991.

Smith, D. (1985). Developing self-advocacy skills in adults with mental retardation. Presentation at the Annual Meeting of the American Association on Mental

Deficiency, May 30, 1985. University Affiliated Cincinnati Center for Developmental Disabilities, Cincinnati, Ohio.

Speaking for Ourselves. (1987). Speaking For Ourselves Bulletin. Plymouth Meeting, PA, November, 1987.

Williams, P., & Shoultz, B. (1982). *We can speak for ourselves: Self-advocacy by mentally handicapped people.* Bloomington: Indiana University press.

Chapter 11

A PLAN TO ELIMINATE STIGMA IN THE MENTAL RETARDATION SYSTEM

. . . What do you do in your job? What do you really do to help us (Edwards, 1982, p. 81)?

I know that you are experts in this field because of your schooling, training . . . and professional experience. I am also an expert in this field because of my firsthand experience: living in institutions and the community, fighting for a good education, getting a real job, searching for good health care, struggling to pay my bills, looking for long-term support, and speaking up for my needs and my rights to lawmakers (Monroe, 1994, p. 10).

. . . You will be an employee of the agency but your main focus will be to provide supports for consumers . . . The consumers have input into your continued employment. If they do not wish for a person to provide services for them, they may request a change of staff (Excerpts from a "consumer-driven" philosophy of Champaign Residential Services, 1995).

A major theme throughout this book is that people with a mental retardation label have numerous capabilities that are overlooked because of the veil of stigma. Most consumers of the mental retardation system, particularly those with a label of mild or moderate mental retardation, have some awareness of the harmful effects of stigma in their lives. Many have taken steps, individually and collectively, to confront the promotion of stigma.

Some labeled people have succeeded in developing friendships and other close ties with people who do not have disabilities, particularly when given the opportunity. Growing numbers are joining self-advocacy groups and representing themselves in ways that could not have been imagined decades ago. Some self-advocates have taken on many new roles including becoming lobbyists, educators and trainers, board members, volunteer counselors, consultants, and researchers.

Stigma in the Mental Retardation System

While this somewhat quiet revolution is going on, the mental retardation system appears to be largely an uninterested bystander or at times even an unintended adversary. Chapter 3 describes many ways in which social agencies and their employees perpetuate stigma. Table 1 in Chapter 3 identifies seven general ways in which stigma is promoted, and the mental retardation system is often guilty of promoting all but one of them. Only extreme derogatory and abusive stigma practices seem largely absent from the System.

In review, the System is often involved in inappropriately using labels and other terminology in referring to their consumers. In many instances, agencies and their staff are insensitive to and often unaware of the disdain that their consumers have for labels like "retarded" or "the mentally retarded." Sadly, these offensive labels are still given high visibility in the identity of many agencies that have not taken seriously the message of the self-advocacy movement, that they are "people first."

Mental retardation agencies are also guilty of age-inappropriateness in their dealings with adult consumers. They refer to adult consumers as "kids" and nonverbally communicate with them in childlike ways, such as a pat on their head. Many programs reveal these biases as well, for example, arts and crafts; games and toys; movies; and parks, playgrounds, and other outings that are more appropriate for children than adults. Some of the restrictions and other means of social control imposed on adult consumers are also a manifestation of age-inappropriateness.

Typically, the System also frequently overlooks the capacity of its consumers to speak for themselves. Agency providers usually speak for their consumers instead of supporting, assisting, and teaching them to speak for themselves. One important example involves case planning. Seldom do consumers assume a significant role in case conferences when their service plans are developed or evaluated, or when major changes are considered in their living or work arrangements.

Actually, many agencies are now involving their consumers in their case conferences, but a way has not often been found to truly hear what many of them are feeling or needing. Perhaps, this difficulty derives from the communication challenges of some people with disabilities, but other barriers are also evident. For example, many staff members do not take the time to hear what consumers have to say, and many times consumers' views are overlooked because they conflict with what the staff think is best.

Another stigma-promoting pattern is to overlook each person's individuality and uniqueness. The population of people labeled with mental retardation is extremely diverse. Yet, programs still seemed canned and designed indiscriminantly for large groups of people. The initial step in an effective program planning process is to determine each consumer's needs; yet, the individual needs of consumers are not a primary factor influencing program designs. For example, in residential services it is quite common to assign a new consumer to an existing "residential slot" that is immediately available rather than creating a new residential arrangement that is uniquely designed for that individual.

The barriers to greater independence in this field are often formidable. Segregated programming is a prime example. Most programs of the System have a pattern of being segregated from the mainstream, which denies people opportunities for greater integration and inclusion. Excessive and inappropriate use of rules and restrictions also serve as barriers to learning how to become more independent. Restrictions are often imposed on consumers without taking into account how they can learn to assume greater responsibility for their lives.

The roles assigned to consumers are also very limiting. People with disabilities are expected to be dependent upon staff, appreciative of what they already have, and accepting of the status quo. Consumers sometimes attempt to break out of these traditional roles; their expressions of anger, criticisms, and defiance can be pleas to try something new. Yet, such behavior may be misinterpreted as noncompliance or evidence of a serious behavior problem. Staff members often need to learn new ways to respond to such expressions and channel them in a positive direction. Most important, new roles must be discovered for consumers, and consumers can help in identifying these roles.

A Plan to Eliminate Stigma

Instead of being a perpetrator of stigma, the mental retardation system and its agencies should be taking the lead in confronting and eliminating this problem. A plan for eliminating stigma in the mental retardation system is proposed, consisting of six major tasks that agencies and professionals are challenged to take on.

1. Work to Eliminate Stigma Identifiers That Are Within the System's Control.

One major problem that needs to be addressed is the mental retardation system's promotion of stigma identifiers. The System and its employees often inadvertently create and foster a wide array of stigma identifiers or symbols that evoke negative reactions toward consumers.

The System is clearly working on this problem. Most agencies have led a concerted effort to reduce their consumers' stigma identifiers that are easily amenable to change. Examples include encouraging consumers to wear socially desirable clothing and to learn good grooming habits. These efforts should be coupled with a more ambitious commitment to minimize stigma identifiers that are more difficult to change. Labels and undeveloped social skills of consumers are two important examples.

The Issue of Labels

The mental retardation label may be the most harmful stigma symbol existing within the System. Many people, particularly those with mild and moderate retardation labels, deny that they are "mentally retarded" even though others perceive them by this label. As was mentioned in earlier chapters, many individuals perceive their disability as a specific, localized condition, such as a learning deficit, slowness, or a physical disability.

Many in the self-advocacy movement not only disavow the mental retardation label but angrily deplore its indiscriminate use by the System. Many staff working in the System insensitively overlook why these people have such distaste for this label. Labeled people often explain that they feel that "mental retardation" is associated with people who are totally dependent or incapable of taking care of themselves.

A less pejorative label would certainly be helpful to the self-esteem of those who are labeled. Perhaps, people who are labeled with mild and moderate retardation could be distinguished from those labeled severely and profoundly retarded. We tend to forget that, in most cases, these two groups have different etiologies for their conditions; the former group most often has an environmental or unknown cause, and the latter group an organic diagnosis (Kurtz, 1977).

Labels may not be needed at all. However, if they are needed, new innovative ones could be considered. Examples used by some agencies include people with "cognitive disabilities," "cognitive challenges," or "intellectual challenges;" and "people with special needs."

Most important, the mental retardation system should listen to labeled people to discern what is acceptable to them. Labeled people prefer other descriptors such as "slower" or "a learning problem." Further, they are consistently reminding us of "people first" language, and they want to be called by their personal names not a label.

Perhaps, an informal process could be established in which national and local self-advocacy groups consider the questions: *What labels and other terms are appropriate in referring to you, and when should these labels be used and not used?* This process could occur every 4–5 years. It should be noted that other minority communities periodically address the question of how they want to be identified. For example, "African American" seems to be currently preferred among people of African descent, while they have previously preferred "Black," and before that, "Negro."

However, merely changing the label will not be a panacea if nothing else changes (Hastings, 1994). A new label may appear to lessen the impact of stigma for awhile, but that label will likely take on pejorative connotations over time. Examples of pejorative labels that were previously acceptable are "imbecile," "moron," and "idiot," and more recently, "mental deficiency" and "handicap." Lasting change will undoubtedly require a fundamental transformation in how we feel about and treat people with disabilities. This transformation is the only long-term solution to overcoming the negative appeal of labels.

Other Stigma Identifiers

Many stigma identifiers are also reflected in agency policies and practices. These identifiers should be targets of change in reducing stigma as well. Agencies should thoroughly scrutinize their policies, programs, and formal and informal staff practices in search of possible identifiers of stigma. Consumers of agencies should become involved in this evaluation process. Examples of questions that agencies and their consumers could ask themselves are:

- Are consumers unnecessarily traveling in large groups when they are in public places?
- Are program provisions varied in response to the diverse needs of consumers?

- Do consumers frequently attend social functions that are attended only by other labeled people?
- Are consumers offered opportunities to associate with nondisabled people who share common interests?
- Do consumers utilize the services of generic agencies and organizations or do they only rely on the services of the mental retardation system?
- Does the mental retardation system give priority to educating generic agencies about the needs of consumers with disabilities?
- Do agencies in the System include the mental retardation label or other identifiers of stigma in their name, on their motor vehicles, buildings, or stationary?
- Do staff members share information about their consumers' disabilities with others when it is not necessary or appropriate?
- Are residential programs in the System offering opportunities for their consumers to visit with neighbors and participate in neighborhood activities?

Other examples of stigma identifiers of this nature are presented in PASSING, a field manual designed for evaluating human service agencies' implementation of normalization goals (Wolfensberger & Thomas, 1983).

2. Be Responsive to Consumers' Attempts to Cope with Stigma.

Chapters 5 and 6 depict the keen awareness of stigma and some of the coping strategies of labeled people. These consumers understand the nature of their disabilities, and they are keenly aware of the stigma identifiers associated with their disabilities. Most disavow being identified as mentally retarded and view this label as a stigma symbol. They have developed varying degrees of sophistication in coping with stigma; some are clever and confident in the way in which they face and manage stigma while others appear more vulnerable and inept. Five specific strategies of coping with stigma were presented in Chapter 6. These strategies and others should be viewed as options that can be considered by labeled people in their attempts to manage and overcome stigma.

The first pattern involves no particular strategy but a beginning attempt to cope with stigma encounters. Labeled people reflecting this pattern are vulnerable and awkward when faced with stigma. These consumers may need assistance with recognizing and more fully understanding the nature of stigma.

Seeking the "positive" aspects of stigma is another strategy used in coping with stigma. It is a strategy that is likely to be fostered without conscious intent and could have negative consequences for consumers' development. As was emphasized in Chapter 6, the community-based mental retardation system offers numerous service benefits that may otherwise be unavailable to consumers. While many of these services promote dignity and greater independence, not all do. The System sometimes unknowingly perpetuates dependency, stigmatization, and unnecessary segregation while rewarding its consumers with secondary "positive" benefits for cooperating.

A most challenging task for the System involves sifting out the elements of policies, programs, and practices that reward consumers for maintaining dependency or the status quo when options exist for greater independence and societal inclusion. Consumers should be enlisted to help with this task, particularly during evaluations of agencies.

"Covering," another strategy, seems to be widely used and supported in the System. This strategy is a very positive one, has applicability for virtually every labeled person, and is noncontroversial. The emphasis in covering is on minimizing the obtrusiveness of stigmatic attributes. Normalization and social role valorization theories provide extensive guidelines for promoting this option (Brown & Smith, 1992; Flynn and Nitsch, 1980; Wolfensberger, 1972; Wolfensberger, 1983).

"Passing," another coping strategy, is based on the willful decision to conceal one's stigmatic identity with the intent of gaining acceptance from nonlabeled people in settings where one's identity is not known. The option of pretending to be a person without a mental retardation label is a controversial element of passing that many staff members may be reluctant to support. Yet, it seems that people who pass are most often disavowing stigma identifiers that have no real positive benefit.

Passing should be considered by the System as a coping strategy that may have merit. Agency personnel who are resistant to considering this option should be helped to reexamine their position. The System should be particularly receptive to assisting with passing if it involves concealing stigma identifiers promoted by its agencies. In my experience, passing is frequently evident as a disavowal of such things as the mental retardation label, affiliations with a mental retardation agency, or associations with a group of people with more stigmatic attributes. All of these are usually agency-promoted stigma identifiers.

Passing is a more controversial option if it involves denying a cognitive or physical attribute in a central area of life like employment, for example concealing one's disability while seeking a new job. In these instances, the moral issue of encouraging people to deliberately conceal an aspect of their identity needs to be considered carefully, particularly in terms of the potential negative consequences for a consumer. Ultimately, the consumers' needs and desires should be a central consideration in determining whether or not to help with passing, as this option could be very beneficial in promoting societal inclusion.

A limiting feature of passing is that it is feasible for only some people who are labeled with mental retardation. It should be noted that passing as a less stigmatic person requires that the person's stigmatic attributes be easily concealable and that the person have an aptitude for managing situations by passing.

A final coping strategy available to labeled people is to directly confront stigma and its perpetrators. Most people with a mental retardation label may not be equipped to confront others and will need assistance in developing the competencies to do it. A capacity to communicate anger appropriately is a necessary aspect of confrontation. In many instances, staff members may have to give labeled people permission to express their anger to overcome many years of social conditioning aimed at restraining it. Help may be needed in identifying internal and external barriers to expressing anger, and learning and rehearsing effective ways of expressing it. Assertiveness training is helpful to introduce in this regard.

3. Encourage and Support "Private Work" in Small Groups.

Small groups are important for labeled people wishing to discuss personal issues related to stigma. (Chapter 9 focuses on the private work that occurs in these groups.) Groups are preferred to individual approaches so that consumers with similar concerns can help each other. Using the concept of the group as "an enterprise in mutual aid," the firsthand experiences of several people with disabilities can be enlisted to help other members solve their problems (Shulman, 1992).

The group facilitator can present pertinent material and offer suggestions to the group members, but primarily encourages the members to help each other. As was explained in earlier chapters, not everyone can be effective in facilitating these special groups. Group facilitators need to be respecting and supportive of consumers as they explore pertinent disability issues; these allies also need to communicate confidence in each consumer's ability and potential to help others.

In many agency settings, a taboo exists about openly discussing people's disabilities in their presence. Lorber (1974) identifies this as a "conspiracy of silence," or an unspoken agreement among helping professionals. This position is based on the view that such open discussions serve no useful purpose and may be damaging. Unfortunately, this view is misguided and furthers consumers' beliefs that their disabilities are too horrible or undesirable to mention.

Agencies and professionals should directly confront this taboo about discussing disabilities by encouraging helpful discussion. Peer groups can provide a supportive atmosphere for consumers to openly talk about themselves, their disabilities, and their problems with stigma. In these discussions, it is vital for consumers to be helped to distinguish the disability-related aspects of their problems from the stigma-related ones. By doing this, they can better understand the causes of stigma that exist outside themselves.

For instance, a disability-related aspect of a speech impediment is manifested as unclear speech that is difficult for others to understand, while the stigma-related aspects could be negative reactions of others, such as showing discomfort or ignoring the person's comments.

Peer groups are also valuable in helping members prepare to face stigma. Various strategies for managing and overcoming stigma can be explored. Role play and other simulation exercises can be introduced to rehearse ways to handle a stigma encounter. Experimentation with these strategies between group sessions can also be encouraged.

4. Seek the Consumers' Voices in Evaluations of Agency Programs.

The voices of labeled people need to be heard through a variety of program evaluations of agencies. Consumer satisfaction studies are a primary way to do this. These studies typically ask the general questions:

- How do the consumers feel about the agency, the services that they are receiving, and the service providers?

- Are the services helping them meet their particular needs?
- In what specific ways are they satisfied and dissatisfied?

I recommend that every agency periodically conduct a consumer satisfaction survey to determine their consumers' degree of satisfaction with their services. One agency has helpful guidelines for conducting these consumer surveys (Champaign Residential Services, Inc. 1995). This agency conducts consumer interviews at least twice each year and in an environment free of coercion. Consumers can select an advocate or guardian to accompany them in the interview, and the program director is assigned responsibility for any necessary follow-up action.

Consumers' positive responses to questions of satisfaction are one important indication of program effectiveness. Other indications of program effectiveness are also needed, such as outcome measures of the consumers' progress. However, if large numbers of consumers are dissatisfied with a program, then it cannot be viewed as successful even if all of the other indicators are positive.

The type of method used to determine consumer satisfaction is critical. In many cases, the views of labeled people cannot be adequately understood solely using standardized interviews, questionnaires, or quasi-experimental designs. Simply asking them questions that have a "yes/no" response, for example, is not likely to elicit what they think and feel. Instead, these questions may lead to acquiescence or the most socially desirable response. To overcome acquiescence, I recommend using qualitative research approaches in combination with standardized measures.

Qualitative research is one of the most effective ways of eliciting the voices of people with a mental retardation label in program evaluations (Edgerton & Langness, 1978; Taylor & Bogdan, 1984). Qualitative research primarily consists of in-depth interviewing or participant-observation approaches. In-depth interviewing involves open-ended questions with probing to elicit clarification and elaboration. The interview is flexibly administered, and the questions are not necessarily asked in a particular order. Participant-observation involves a more extended period of study involving relatively unobtrusive observation and participation in the lives of subjects. In-depth interviewing methods are also used with participant-observation.

Qualitative research has long been the predominant research approach used by anthropologists and some sociologists as they have attempted to communicate across cultures to people in the non-Western world. This approach is useful with labeled people because it is recognized that they, in a sense, may come from a different culture and speak a different "language." This approach helps us to communicate with labeled people across these social and language barriers.

One distinguishing characteristic of qualitative research is that the researcher attempts to explore and balance "two perspectives" from the data, one through the subject's eyes and the other through the researcher's eyes. In the former, the researcher must learn how to perceive and experience the subject's world as the subject does. These findings are often useful because they reveal what it is actually like to be "in the shoes" of a person with a special attribute or condition. Examples of consumer satisfaction questions can be found in various studies (e.g., Dudley, Ahlgrim-Delzell, & Conroy, 1995).

Program evaluation questions could directly focus on stigma issues. Consumers could be asked questions about various types of stigma that may be fostered by the System, such as:

1. How do you feel about the term, "mental retardation?" Do you think that this term should be used to identify consumers in the agency? Explain why or why not.
2. Does the service (specify which one) that you receive meet your needs? How does this service help you? How could it be more helpful to you? Are there other services that you would rather receive?
3. Do staff listen to you or ignore you when you talk? (If "ignore," ask for an explanation.)
4. Do staff treat you like an adult or a child? (If "child," ask for an explanation.)
5. Did you pick this job or did someone pick it for you? (Explore how they feel if they responded "someone picked it for you.")
6. Do you want to keep this job or pick another one? (Explore their concerns and desires if they want to pick another job.)
7. Do you have enough privacy? (If not, explore their concerns.)

5. Work Closely with the Self-Advocacy Movement

I believe that the mental retardation system should be giving more attention to voices in the self-advocacy movement? A description of this movement and some of its goals and activities are the focus of Chapter

10. These self-advocates have expressed many profound and stirring messages about their problems, hopes, and dreams. These messages emanate from their conventions, local self-advocacy groups, and various publications written by them and others (e.g., President's Committee on Mental Retardation, 1994).

Most of the self-advocates' concerns seem to be problems pertinent to the mental retardation system. Self-advocates have made numerous recommendations for enhancing the delivery system that serves them (Cone, 1994; Longhurst, 1994; People First of Washington, 1985; Shapiro, 1991; Speaking for Ourselves, 1990). Some examples are to discontinue using labels that they perceive as harmful, close institutions, and support more independent community living. They want more choices in employment, where to live, developing relationships, and making other decisions affecting them. They are interested in changing guardianship laws, and they want fair wages for their work. Some also complain that buildings and transportation are not physically accessible to them.

Several recommendations have been made in Chapter 10 for how the System can give greater support to the self-advocacy movement, particularly in encouraging greater consumer involvement. Suggestions are also given for involving staff members in self-advocacy as allies.

6: Offer Opportunities for Consumers to Assume Empowering Roles

Some labeled people are ready to break out of traditional consumer roles that characterize them as passive recipients of service. In place of these roles, they wish to take on new roles that involve more responsibility and risk-taking. These new roles can be "empowering" because they result in people assuming more control over their lives.

Consumers often give cues about new roles that they desire, even though their messages may be indirect and subtle. For example, consumers in a counseling relationship could appear resistant to help when what they want is less advice from the counselor and more control over selection of topics and the flow of communication. Or consumers may complain about the way that their agency advertises itself because they wish to help with publicity drives, fund raising, or community education efforts.

There is no ready made-list of new roles to consider. Some roles are quite common and relevant to many social situations, while other roles may be unusual or even unique to a particular consumer. A few general examples of roles are offered.

Advocacy

Advocacy has already been discussed as an empowering role in Chapter 10. Advocacy could focus on one's own rights or the rights of a group of consumers. The self-advocacy movement may be the best place to learn about this role. Agencies may want to hire consumers who are especially effective advocates to assist other consumers in speaking for themselves. For example, consumer advocates could assist other consumers in speaking out in their case conferences.

Helping Others

A desire to help other people is frequently expressed among labeled people. Many people have a deep desire to assume such a role. In some cases, this desire derives from an appreciation for the help that they have received; they want to return the favor by helping others. Or they may identify with a staff person who models a good helper. Also, many perceive helping others as a way of being a good United States citizen.

Many helping roles are possible within and outside the System. A consumer may be able to do peer counseling, speak to other consumers on a topic of expertise, teach a specific skill, or share the coleadership of a group with a staff member. While these examples involve helping other labeled people, providing help to nonlabeled people or a neighborhood group could also be considered. Examples include doing fund raising for the Red Cross, volunteering to help with a neighborhood clean-up campaign, and participating on a social ministry committee of a church or synagogue. In some of these instances, the role may be a volunteer one, while other roles should involve remuneration to convey the value of the person's contribution.

Despite the many good reasons why labeled people may want to help others, many staff members are not sensitive to this need. Eugene is a good example (Dudley, 1983). As mentioned in Chapter 3, Eugene wanted to entertain children with physical disabilities in a nearby hospital. His reason was, "I'm thankful I can see, hear, talk, cross my hands, and cross my legs. I'm thankful. That's why I want to help out other people." He spent an entire year trying to persuade staff to help him, but no one took him seriously.

Training Role

I have found that labeled people who are especially articulate can effectively assume a cotraining role with professionals who are conducting community education or staff training. When I have conducted staff training sessions on stigma, for example, I have usually involved a labeled person to work with me.

One training model that I have developed is called "dyad exchanges on stigma." It fosters communication about stigma problems between staff members and consumers. This training model involves two sessions, one with staff members and the second one with dyads of staff members and consumers. These groups are usually limited to 10 to 15 people.

The first session for staff members is devoted to a presentation of the problem of stigma, its manifestations in agencies, and the stigma awareness and coping strategies of consumers. The objective is to thoroughly familiarize these staff members with the problem of stigma. My coleader usually discusses this topic in more informal ways and shares personal encounters with stigma that have occurred in her agency.

Staff members who attend the first training session are asked to bring one of their consumers to the second session. They are asked to select a fairly articulate consumer with whom they have some rapport. The second session begins with a brief introduction of stigma. Consumers are assigned a consultant role in the group and are identified as the "experts," while staff are encouraged to be "recipients of knowledge."

After some general preparation, each dyad has private time to discuss the topic of stigma. Consumers share their concerns about stigma occurring at their agency. Staff members are expected to primarily ask questions and listen. After these discussions, all of the dyads return to the group and discuss what they have learned. The coleaders use this time to give positive reinforcement to any breakthroughs occurring in these private discussions.

In one such training session, excerpts of the session illustrate some breakthroughs. After the dyads returned to the group to share what they had discussed, one consumer made a passionate plea for removing unnecessary agency restrictions on her whereabouts. She read a letter that she intended to send to her residential director. Another consumer who has lived in an institution for 16 years cautiously complained that her money was withheld from her because she did not lose the weight that was prescribed for her. The coleader of this training session, a formerly labeled person, shared an earlier personal experience in which she had to adapt to a similarly restrictive environment in a community group home. This coleader explained that the house rules were helpful to her even though she did not like them; she eventually wanted more independence and now lives on her own. Her comments had a major impact on the participants in the training session and could not have been contributed by the professional who was her coleader.

Research Role

Some labeled people have demonstrated an ability to conduct research studies on topics of concern to agencies (e.g., People First of California, 1984). Studies of consumer satisfaction, for example, could be done by labeled people who interview other consumers. A simple interview format could be devised with the help of a research consultant. The interviewers would need training in their role.

A description of a research study conducted by a group of labeled people illustrates some of the issues involved in this role (Friedman, 1985). A project team of six interviewers were trained to interview 100 consumers in a sheltered workshop. The purpose of these interviews was to explore how the consumers felt about their jobs at the workshop. All of the interviews were taped.

The interviewers were officers of a local self-advocacy organization. They assumed their new roles with pride and a heightened sense of self-esteem. To the surprise of many, they demonstrated an impressive sense of competency in what they were doing. Further, they succeeded despite some unanticipated obstacles that were imposed by their workshop supervisors who were reluctant to give them permission to take a brief leave of absence from their jobs.

Three of the interviewers could not read, which posed another obstacle. They were given the questions on a tape and asked to practice in role plays and on their own. When they conducted the interviews, they would listen to each question on earphones and then repeat it to the interviewees. The other interviewers and the research consultants provided lots of support to them, which assured their success.

All but one of the questions that the interviewers asked were close-ended and the interviewee was to choose a response from a set of response categories. One open-ended question at the end of the interview asked for comments. During the first few interviews, consumers expressed fear that their staff might not like what they had to say. The interviewers emphasized confidentiality and also decided to add a question in the interview about whether or not consumers had fears of repercussions from staff members or others. About half of the people who were asked this question expressed such fears.

These interviewers found that most of the consumers wanted a job outside the workshop but many also expressed fears about some of the unknown aspects of outside work. Most also found the workshop to be satisfactory and found their jobs to be easy to do. Many also gave open-ended responses about the workshop such as "I like this place." and "It's fun."

Policy Board Members

Another important role is to be a board member of an agency and have input into its policy-making decisions. Many organizations have appointed labeled people to their boards, including state developmental disabilities councils, governmental bodies, and local agencies. One of the best examples is the recent decision by the President of the United States to appoint two labeled people to the prestigious President's Committee on Mental Retardation for the first time in its history.

Unfortunately, these board member roles are often only a "token" of participation and do not involve consumer input that is taken seriously. This may be due to several factors. The agenda of board meetings may not seem understandable or relevant to the person with a disability. Or the labeled person may be intimidated by the other board members who are more articulate. This person may not be able to think or speak as quickly as the others, and may feel outnumbered and isolated. Also, often no one is present at board meetings as a coach or facilitator. In general, a power imbalance exists.

I have a few suggestions for increasing the balance of power between labeled people on boards and other board members:

Mutual Support System: If labeled people are appointed to a policy board, include two or more such people and help them to develop a mutual support system. Usually one labeled person on a board feels isolated and has no one to talk to privately about these meetings. Such circumstances often result in the person focusing on winning the approval of the other board members or simply withdrawing in silence.

Board Training: The labeled people on a board will need training before joining the board and while they are serving as members. Other policy board members will also benefit from some training for this new "partnership" with labeled people. The other board members may need to learn how to listen and truly hear the concerns of the people with disabilities. Also, they may need help in learning how to respond positively to the suggestions of labeled members so that their ideas will have a better chance of being implemented.

Caucusing after Meetings: One specific approach that can be used is to encourage labeled people on the board to caucus with each other after meetings and share the results of their caucus session at the next meeting. These board members can discuss the topic among themselves, with or without an ally. They can take the time needed to think through the responses that they would like to make. They may also wish to consult their consumer groups for ideas, and they may want to be briefed by an expert on a topic with which they are not familiar. While caucusing may be a helpful additional step to take, particularly in the early stages of their membership, it should not prevent these members from spontaneously participating in board meetings when topics arise.

Consumer Advisory Board

Another important role is to be a member of a consumer advisory group that advises the organization's decision-makers on particular issues. These recipients of service essentially become "advisors" to a policy board or executive director. They can represent a larger consumer constituency group that elects them.

These advisory board members will need training and ongoing support from an ally. Their relationship to the policy board will need to be explicitly defined, with concrete mechanisms worked out for how their input can influence policy making decisions.

The policy board or executive director could present the advisory group with questions or topics that need consumer feedback. Examples of topics include evaluating the strengths and limitations of an existing program or considering the need for a new program. The advisory board would deliberate and caucus in private on these topics. With the help of an ally, they could share all of their views with each other and attempt to arrive at a clearly articulated collective position to be presented to the policy board.

Existing informal groups within agencies could also serve as ad hoc consumer advisory groups. Ad hoc groups in sheltered workshops are an example. Many groups meet in sheltered workshop programs during coffee breaks, lunch periods, and other nonwork periods (Dudley &

Schatz, 1985). The informal discussions and exchanges of opinions in these groups could be a valuable source of ideas. Staff members could ask to join these discussions to hear the consumers' ideas and facilitate more focused conversations on topics of concern to the agency.

The local self-advocacy groups may also be willing to become ad hoc advisory groups on particular topics. As was mentioned earlier, self-advocacy groups are usually not taken very seriously by the mental retardation system. Yet, self-advocates spend an enormous amount of time and energy learning how to communicate with each other, cultivating representative democracy, and developing positions on issues pertinent to agencies. Agency administrators could ask the leaders of this movement, for example, to offer workshops at self-advocacy conventions that would address general topics of concern to agencies.

References

Brown, H., and Smith, H. (Eds.) (1992). *Normalisation: A reader for the nineties.* New York: Tavistock/Routledge.

Champaign Residential Services (1995). Verification of consumer-driven philosophy. Champaign Residential Services, Urbana, Ohio.

Cone, A. (1994). Reflections on self-advocacy: Voices for choices. *Mental Retardation, 32,* (6), 444–445.

Dudley, J. (1983). *Living with stigma: The plight of the people who we label mentally retarded.* Springfield, IL: Charles C Thomas.

Dudley, J., Ahlgrim-Delzell, L., & Conroy, J. (1995). Investigating the satisfaction of *Thomas S.* class members in Year 1 & 2: Intermediate findings of two subgroups of class members with and without implemented plans, Monograph 5, Charlotte, NC: *Thomas S.* Longitudinal Research Study, University of North Carolina at Charlotte, August, 1995.

Dudley, J., & Schatz, M. (1985). The missing link in evaluating sheltered workshops: The clients' input. *Mental Retardation, 23*(5), 235–240.

Edgerton, R., & Langness, L. (1978). Observing mentally retarded persons in community settings: An anthropological perspective. In Sackett, G. (Ed.). *Observing behavior, Volume 1: Theory and applications in mental retardation.* Baltimore: University Park Press.

Edwards, J. (1982). *We are people first: Our handicaps are secondary.* Portland: Ednick.

Flynn, R., & Nitsch, K. (1980). *Normalization, social integration, and community services.* Baltimore: University Park Press.

Friedman, M. (1985). Report on sheltered workshop interviews by consumer data collectors. Evaluation and Research Group, Temple University, Developmental Disabilities Center, Philadelphia PA, October, 1985.

Hastings, R. (1994). On "good" terms: Labeling people with mental retardation. *Mental Retardation, 32* (5), 363–365.

Kurtz, R. (1977). *Social aspects of mental retardation.* Toronto: Lexington Books.

Longhurst, N. (1994). *The self-advocacy movement by people with developmental disabilities: A demographic study and directory of self-advocacy groups in the United States.* Washington, D.C.: American Association on Mental Retardation.

Lorber, M. (1974). *Consulting the mentally retarded: An approach to the definition of mental retardation by experts.* Unpublished doctoral dissertation, University of California at Los Angeles.

Monroe, T. (1994). Self-advocate's perspective. In President's Committee on Mental Retardation, *The national reform agenda and people with mental retardation: Putting people first,* pp. 9–10. Washington, D.C.: U.S. Department of Health and Human Services, April, 1994.

People First of California. (1984). *Surviving in the system: Mental retardation and the retarding environment.* Sacramento: California State Council on Developmental Disabilities.

People First of Washington. (1985). *Speaking up and speaking out: An international self-advocacy movement.* Tacoma, WA: Report of the International Self-Advocacy Leadership Conference, July, 1984.

President's Committee on Mental Retardation, *The national reform agenda and people with mental retardation: Putting people first,* Washington, D.C.: U.S. Department of Health and Human Services, April, 1994.

Shapiro, J. (1991). Pity is a four-letter word. *Fellowship Magazine,* September, 1991.

Shulman, L. (1992). *The skills of helping: Individuals, families, and groups,* 3rd ed. Itasca, IL: F.E. Peacock.

Speaking for Ourselves. (1990). Speaking For Ourselves Bulletin: A newsletter for and by our members and friends. Volume 1, Issue 1, Plymouth Meeting, PA, June, 1990.

Taylor, S., & Bogdan, R. (1984). *Introduction to qualitative research methods: The search for meanings.* (Second Edition). New York: John Wiley & Sons.

Wolfensberger, W. (1972). *The principle of normalization in human services.* Toronto: National Institute on Mental Retardation.

Wolfensberger, W. (1983). Social role valorization: A proposed new term for the principle of normalization. *Mental Retardation, 21*(6), 234–239.

Wolfensberger, W., & Thomas, S. (1983). *PASSING (Program Analysis of Service Systems' Implementation of Normalization Goals): Normalization criteria and ratings manual* (2nd ed.) Toronto: National Institute on Mental Retardation.

Chapter 12

LEAVING THE MENTALLY RETARDED WORLD

A Maine consumer: "Society does things to us and for us. I want to do things for myself. I want society to support my role as a functioning member (Jaskulski, Metzler, & Zierman, 1990, p. 197)."

Interviewer: "What has been your biggest problem since you learned you weren't retarded?"

John: "Being on my own. I don't think I can handle it" (Edgerton, 1986, p. 120).

Labeled people live within a mentally retarded world. If they want to leave it, they must contend with the "wall" of stigma in their lives, described in Chapter 4. This wall has been erected by society, and it is sometimes perpetuated by the mental retardation system.

The wall does have latent social purposes. It is intended by some to protect labeled people from the risks and dangers in society, and it is intended by others to minimize the "intrusion" of labeled people in the lives of people in the outside world.

Efforts to break out of this confined world are fraught with problems. First, there is resistance from labeled people and others in their support system. Further, the System usually does not help its consumers to leave. If labeled people are fortunate enough to leave on their own, they come to realize that they must stay out. They have no alternative but to disassociate themselves from the people in the world left behind.

There seems to be no established portal for labeled people through the wall. While society has developed a means of labeling them and socializing them into a mentally retarded world, the methods for removing the label and resocializing them to be "nonmentally retarded" are largely nonexistent. Those who want to leave need substantial help, which is the focus of this chapter.

171

The Leavers

Goffman (1963) describes the final phase of "passing" as one in which passing encompasses all aspects of a person's life. The secret of having a stigmatic identity is known only to the passer and possibly to a few additional people who assist in the concealment. In this phase, a person who has been labeled with mental retardation and has lived in the mentally retarded world would be in a position to leave it.

Who are the people in this final phase of "passing" who can leave the mental retardation system? Edgerton (1986) points out that many of them are people who in the past had low IQs and were institutionalized; later they were found to have IQs that were average or higher. Their incorrect intelligence scores were found to be due to cultural differences, deafness, emotional and behavioral problems, or other factors. The number of people with these circumstances could be in the tens of thousands.

Other people may be ready to leave the System based on an increasing competence that they have developed over the years. Most of them likely have been diagnosed with "mild retardation" and have relatively high adaptive behavior scores. Semi-independent living arrangements, supported employment, other services of the System, and the self-advocacy movement have all been instrumental in increasing their competence, self-confidence, and capacity to develop associations outside the System.

A third group of labeled people may be forced to leave the System. With increasing threats to governmental funding and a shift to more stringent standards of eligibility, growing numbers of higher-functioning labeled people could have their services abruptly terminated. Countless others have already been phased out of service provisions to address budget deficits and to make room for people with greater needs.

The System's Complicity

The mental retardation system meets many basic needs of its consumers. Undoubtedly, most labeled people would have real difficulty surviving if the System did not exist. However, some labeled people no longer need its services or the services are no longer relevant to their needs.

Consumers who function at higher levels, in particular, have a capacity to live more independently and assume more normalized roles. Many are employed in regular jobs outside the System. They have been able to develop close associations with their neighbors and other "outsiders." Some maintain committed intimate relationships, succeed in marital relationships, and assume parental roles. And many can creatively cope with the stigma in their lives by passing, covering, and confronting these problems.

Also, numerous natural supports in the community can, at times, replace services of the System. Friendships have been found in churches, clubs, neighborhood groups, work sites, and other places in the community. These community groups also offer many of the services provided by the System, including social contact, intellectual stimulation, tangible aid and advice, and emotional support. In some cases, consumers even prefer these natural supports to those of the System.

As was pointed out in Chapter 11, the mental retardation system often seems unaware of the abilities and potentials of many of its consumers. Too often the System neglects to prepare consumers with competencies and survival skills needed in the outside world. Further, the System has a pattern of overlooking the potential role of natural supports in the community.

In this chapter, we consider ways to assist consumers in leaving the mental retardation system when they are ready to leave. These consumers can be identified by an assessment process that involves their input. Special programs can be offered to facilitate a successful transition to the "normal world." These programs can also help them become psychologically disengaged from a mental retardation identity.

A Case of Delabeling

The delabeling process involves more than simply removing a label. It involves taking away an important aspect of identity, however debilitating. Excerpts from a research interview with John reveal what this change could mean to a delabeled person (Edgerton, 1986, p. 120):

Interviewer:	"What problems did you have making the transition from being retarded to being a normal person?"
John:	"I tried to act more mature, which was very hard. Still is very hard. I hadn't really grown-up. I was below most people in maturity."
Interviewer:	"Is it easier being retarded?"
John:	"Yeah, you better believe it. You're sheltered you know,

you don't have to take on the responsibility of an adult and everyone, I think, wants to be sheltered. I mean, once in a while. Once in a month I just want to . . . when I have problems I can't cope with I say, 'John, let's go back where I was and act like a little kid again.' "

Interviewer: "What has been the biggest problem since you learned you weren't retarded?"

John: "Being on my own. I don't think I can handle it."

Interviewer: "Did you ever think before about what it would be like to not be retarded, before they told you (that you) weren't retarded?"

John: "No."

Interviewer: "You just accepted it (the label)?"

John: "Yeah, simple, I could take it."

Interviewer: "Do you find it makes a difference in how people think of you?"

John: "Yeah, some people, they put me on a pedestal and say, 'Hey, he's retarded, leave him alone, don't bother him.' When they don't know that I'm retarded, they act like I know how to cope with life. Makes me feel good but other times it freaks me completely out. I think, 'How am I supposed to act now?' If I flub up now I may as well hang it up for good."

John reminds us that delabeling is not simply the removal of a label from one's identity. The delabeling process, while positive, is traumatizing to John and others. A life-time of socialization by the System and family members has taught them to remain incompetent by restricting access to normal experiences and by reinforcing dependency (Edgerton, 1986). Suddenly, they are expected to be different and this involves undoing much of what they have internalized in the past.

After one year without the label, John was expected to achieve his goals—independent living, self-support, and social competence. But did he? Not at all. His many years of socialization could not be erased by simply closing his file.

The System must be responsive to the "leavers" if they are to succeed in the outside world. To help, the System must radically change its approach. Its first goal must be to help undo many years of internalized dependency and incompetence, which may take several years to do.

A Case of People Ready to Leave

In my earlier study (Dudley, 1983), five of the 27 research subjects seemed ready to leave the mental retardation system. All five people were affiliated with a recreation agency serving labeled people. While most of the subjects were noticeably discontented with life in their confined world, these five people seemed especially ready to leave it. Four of them (Nancy, Roger, Karen, and Janet) had an active consumer status with the System, while one (Noreen) had an inactive status. A closer examination of these five subjects sheds some light on who may be ready to leave.

Three overall characteristics seem to capture the circumstances of these subjects. *First, the awareness of stigma that almost all of the subjects of the study revealed seemed intensified for these five subjects.* They expressed more discomfort with their circumstances than the others, and they seemed particularly preoccupied with stratification issues. They often went out of their way to inform others that they were superior to and quite different from peers who were more dependent and stigmatized.

In addition, they had a greater tendency than the others to avoid contact with more stigmatized consumers, particularly in public places. This tendency apparently reflected an intensified alienation of their stigmatic status, with these peers being a painful reminder of it.

Second, these five subjects were more involved in the non-mentally retarded world than the other subjects. All five held jobs outside the System and occasionally frequented outside social clubs for entertainment. They also associated with nonlabeled people outside the System.

These five people identified nonlabeled people as friends more frequently than the other subjects, and they seemed to have more success in establishing such relationships. Noreen had the most success with developing outside relationships and had already discontinued her friendships with consumers at her agency. She had done this by deciding not to return to where these friendships were fostered.

The third distinguishing characteristic of these five subjects is that they appeared and behaved more "normal" than the others. They were not necessarily more intelligent. Essentially, their stigma identifiers were less evident and they could pass more easily in places where they were unknown.

For these five subjects, there appeared to be no special help provided by the System for disengaging. Noreen, who had already left her social agency, worked out her exit by building a beginning support system in the "normal world" and then, upon succeeding, simply abandoned her agency and its world. Janet was planning to leave by secretly arranging a wedding to a man who was living independently.

The move from a group home to a semi-independent apartment was intended as part of an exit plan by Karen, who realized that she could become much more independent of the mental retardation system and staff by living in an apartment. The System supported this plan without fully realizing why it was so important to her.

Transitional Programs to the "Outside World"

The mental retardation system can help people who are ready for delabeling by offering them a distinct set of services. Two interrelated goals of these services would be to disengage from the System and become integrated in the community.

A team could be organized to both provide and coordinate services that are needed. This team could include representatives of agencies from both the mental retardation system and generic organizations in the community. Examples of generic organizations include the YMCA/ YWCA, ecumenical church and synagogue groups, environmental groups, the Junior League, women's circles, fraternal groups like the Kiwanis Club and the Masons, community colleges, and community relations offices of governmental agencies or corporations. Individual volunteers, including formerly labeled people, neighbors, citizen advocates, and others could also be enlisted to be part of the team.

The people selected to work with consumers wanting to leave the System will need to be fully committed to the goal of societal inclusion. Also, these allies will need to develop a special sensitivity to the circumstances of these consumers, including an understanding of their stigma problems and the emotional effects. For example, allies may have difficulty accepting the growing intolerance that these consumers may have for the System and peers who are more stigmatized. Nevertheless, their intolerance, while possibly problematic for others, may be very important in motivating them to want to the leave the System.

Components of a Transitional Program

A transitional program would include a **peer support group** as a central component. This group would meet regularly and offer the members opportunities for problem-solving and support. The nature of the group and the role of the group facilitator(s) would be similar to the peer groups described in Chapter 9. The facilitator would encourage the group members to discuss their concerns with stigma and help them disengage from the System.

The peer group could be cofacilitated by a staff member of the System and a community member. The community member could be a representative of a generic organization or a formerly labeled person successfully integrated in the community. Self-advocacy leaders, in particular, could be good group facilitators.

Opportunities for community linkages should also be created to help these transitional consumers make important connections with the community. For example, these consumers could be encouraged to arrange community outings of interest to them, and the peer group could help them work out these arrangements. Also, transitional consumers could be introduced to community volunteers who would share quality time with them and participate with them in activities of common interest. These volunteers could accompany them to social clubs, churches, or other places to meet new people.

Positive incentives must be built into a transitional program. Generally, the benefits of this program must be perceived by eligible consumers to exceed the benefits of the traditional services that they would leave behind. Specifically, some type of agreement could be reached for discontinuing the traditional services of the System that would no longer be needed.

Identifying Participants

Who would be appropriate participants for a transitional program and how could they be selected? The target group would be the consumer population that has a potential for leaving the mental retardation system. Initially, all eligible consumers could be informed about this program so that they could decide for themselves whether or not they want to become participants.

The consumers selected for this program are likely to be similar to the five subjects described above who were ready to leave (Dudley, 1983). They may be employed on the outside or preparing for that possibility; living semi-independently, living on their own, or desiring such an arrangement; associating fairly comfortably with people in the outside world; and frequenting restaurants, movie theaters, and cultural events in the community.

Their stigma identifiers will likely be minimally noticed or easily managed and concealed. Like the five subjects, some of these consumers may feel increasing discomfort with their peers who are more dependent or stigmatized or both. Their desire may be to associate with others who are more like them as well as individuals who do not have disabilities.

An Illustration

The transitional project illustrated below was developed by a university and a recreation agency serving labeled people. The major components of the project were a peer support group and a "contact person" assigned to each transitional consumer in the community.

Goals: The long-range goal of this project was to help a group of nine labeled people, hereafter referred to as "participants," become more socially integrated in the outside world. Several short-range goals were also identified. The participants of the project were expected to increase their contact with outside people, organizations, and resources. They were also encouraged to develop closer ties with each other, particularly to help each other with integration efforts. For example, pairs of participants were encouraged to explore community resources together.

Another short-term goal was to significantly diminish or discontinue their dependence on their mental retardation agency beyond this transitional project. A specific agreement was worked out whereby the participants could use a traditional service of their agency only if they could explain how this service was needed and not available to them through the transitional project.

Initial Explorations and Contract: The success of the project depended upon the full understanding and cooperation of the nine transitional consumers and their families. The two project coordinators initially interviewed all prospective participants. The program was thoroughly described and discussed with them. They were told that if they chose to participate, they would be expected to agree to discontinue using the other services of their agency while the project was running, and to regularly participate in all aspects of the transitional project. Specific expectations included identifying and working on their personal goals related to the project's purpose, attending all peer group sessions, and using the community contact people who would be available to each of them.

Parents of the participants were also introduced to the project in instances when they were still actively involved. Because we knew how much influence these parents still had over their labeled family member, we did all that we could to gain their full cooperation. Parents were informed about the project's goals of community inclusion and disengagement from the System. Also, considerable time was allowed for parents to thoroughly discuss their questions and reservations.

Identifying Personal Goals: Each participant initially met with one of the project coordinators to begin the process of identifying his or her personal goals pertinent to integration. The goals were also discussed in the peer group sessions, and members were periodically asked to evaluate their success in meeting them. These individualized goals became a focal point for each member to work on throughout the project. Members were also encouraged and helped to modify their goals if they were not feasible.

The participants' goals varied. They identified personal goals that would make them more passable in appearance and interpersonal exchanges. Examples include learning how to use make-up and developing conversation skills with new acquaintances. Some of those who lived with their parents wanted to explore ways to become more independent of them. One participant living at home identified learning how to drive as a short-term goal and moving out of his parents' home as a long-term goal. Other goals were to seek more normalized work and to utilize recreational and leisure activities in the community.

Contact Person: Along with the peer group, each participant was matched with a person who was considered a "contact person." These contact people were university students who agreed to participate in the project. In retrospect, it probably would have been better if they were volunteers from the community.

In general, the role of the contact person was to get together with the participant and do things in the community about every two weeks. Specific activities were usually determined by each participant, with input from the contact person. Conversations were also encouraged, including discussing how the participants could reach their personal goals. Contact people were asked to keep periodic contact with the project coordinators, who were also the facilitators of the peer group, to share pertinent information.

The participants were encouraged to help in defining their contact person's role. Most agreed that the contact person would be like a "buddy." One participant wanted the contact person to help her feel more self-confident by doing things together. One participant wanted his contact person to help him in meeting women. Another wanted to go shopping together because she had little experience with this. Finally, one participant wanted help with finding a better job and hoped her contact person would assist her in some way.

The contact people initially met with the project coordinators to become informed about the project and their particular role. This meeting was followed by an informal gathering in which all of the contact people and participants met and got acquainted. Based on this gathering, participants suggested who they preferred as a contact person, and their choices were honored whenever possible.

Peer Support Group: The nine participants met as a peer group on a weekly basis. They met at a community college rather than at the agency to support the goal of societal inclusion. These group meetings had several purposes. One purpose was for the participants to plan their own excursions to dinner theaters, sports events, concerts, and other places that they wanted to attend. The members decided where they wanted to go, made their own plans and reservations, and chose a companion or two to join them. Subsequent group sessions were used to share and evaluate these experiences and to give feedback on their achievements. In the meantime, the members were discouraged from attending the social events sponsored by their agency.

Another purpose of the group was to work on personal issues. In early group sessions, members were asked to identify as many of their strengths and challenges as possible. The other group members helped each member with this exercise. One member, for example, identified his strengths as mowing the lawn, using public transportation, liking movies and sports, having a charge account, and having a good friend. His challenges or needs included being shy, wanting to be more sociable, wanting to learn how to express himself better, and not being assertive. This exercise helped members to become better acquainted with each other, enhanced their self-confidence, and helped them identify goals to work on.

Evaluations: Informal reflections were encouraged about the participants' progress throughout the project in conversations among the project coordinators, contact persons, and participants. In addition, a more formal evaluation occurred near the end of the project. Participants filled out an evaluation form and shared some of their responses in the group.

In the final evaluation, participants were asked to identify what they had learned. Some of the things that they shared included "how to speak out my words," "how to get along with people," "nothing," and "buying fashionable glasses." Some of the personal achievements that they shared were learning to put on make-up, buying more fashionable clothes, and styling hair. One participant gained insights about herself and another gained self-confidence. One learned to get around the city, and another learned to speak out. Another member who had a tendency to become defensive and hostile when confronted with his limitations was helped to be calmer and self-reflective.

When asked to identify what they liked the best about the peer group, participants said, "I liked telling it like it is," " . . . helped me to listen to myself when I spoke," and "getting out with people." Some enjoyed the discussions on specific topics. They usually commented that they liked their contact person and the time spent together. One commented: "We really got along together. We went skating a few times . . . we called each other and talked."

Things that they did not like included: "The group met too often," and "I didn't like being asked if I called my contact person over and over." One said she did not like being asked personal questions. One member said that he wanted more time with his contact person and more activities together. Another said that her contact person was too busy. Two of the nine participants dropped out of the project before it was over. Both said that they decided that they did not need it, and it was evident that the father of one of them helped her make her decision.

These evaluation comments were made at the end of this project, about nine months after it began. No one had accomplished major changes like moving from a family home or completely disengaging from their agency. Nor was there substantial headway evident in their new connections in the community. Many of these larger achievements were still ahead of them, and much more help would be needed before many of them could completely succeed in the outside world.

Unfortunately, support for this transitional project was available for only nine months. While the project was responsible for some minor changes in the participants' lives, it needed to function for a longer period to accomplish its long-term goals. This realization leads me to strongly recommend that future transitional programs be planned for at least 2 to 3 years to accomplish the goals of System disengagement and community inclusion. In this regard, a strong commitment is needed from sponsoring agencies to insure that such a project can be sustained for that period of time.

Considering Another Strategy in Leaving

Since passing is a feasible option for only some people labeled with mental retardation, what options are left for others who will never be able to conceal or minimize their stigma identifiers? Are they destined to remain in a world of restricted associations, segregated social settings, and limited opportunities? Or is it possible to lower the wall that divides them from the "normal" world?

It is the thesis of this book that all labeled people have a potential role to play in both lowering and dismantling the wall. They have options to choose that can reduce the stigma in their lives, and nonlabeled people who are allies have a significant part to play in assisting them.

Goffman (1963, p. 100) suggests that stigmatized people have another option that has not been mentioned; they can voluntarily disclose the stigmatic attributes of their identity to others. This option may be a phase beyond passing in which labeled people realize that they respect and accept themselves and have no further need to conceal their disability.

In this case, for example, labeled people could approach a stranger on the street and inform the stranger of their cognitive need for assistance without embarrassment. Similarly, they could join a church or a social club and openly identify their disability as an aspect of their identity. Or they could make friends with others and openly inform them of their "label" because it would not affect the new friendship.

After all, the message of this book is that these people should not be ashamed of their disabilities. Their disabilities are a part of who they are. Most important, their disabilities are only ONE part of who they are.

However, the stigma that is associated with their disabilities is also very powerful and problematic. As long as this is the case, it does not seem realistic to encourage people to be so open about this aspect of their identity if they want to be accepted.

A hopeful note to close on is that someday, after significantly more success has occurred in confronting and eliminating stigma, labeled people can "come out" and be accepted members of our society. Steve's comments at a self-advocacy convention reflect his dream of such a society (Dorsey, 1985):

> We can go as far as you allow us to go. We can go as far as we allow ourselves to go. So if we work together, who knows how far hand in hand we can travel together? . . . Put out your hand of help. We need it.

References

Dorsey, S. (1985). "Being handicapped. News Line, Vol. 2, No. 4. Elwyn, PA: Elwyn Institutes, July, 1985.

Dudley, J. (1983). Living with stigma: The plight of the people who we label mentally retarded. Springfield, IL: Charles C Thomas.

Edgerton, R. (1986). A case of delabeling: Some practical and theoretical implications. In L. Langness & H. Levine (Eds.), *Culture and retardation: Life histories of mildly mentally retarded persons in American society,* pp. 101–126. Boston: D. Reidel.

Goffman, E. (1963). Stigma: Notes on the management of spoiled identity. Englewood Cliffs, NJ: Prentice-Hall.

Jaskulski, T., Metzler, C., & Zierman, S. (1990). The 1990 reports: Forging a new era. Washington, D.C.: National Association of Developmental Disabilities Council, May, 1990.

EPILOGUE

John Patrick: Never again should we fall into the practice of neglecting others . . .
Never again should we tolerate injustice toward others without speaking out . . .
Never again should we fail to listen to the people we serve . . . (Graney, 1996,
p. 272).

In retrospect, I am bewildered by how much work still remains to be done to overcome stigma. At the same time, I am mindful that some exceptional work has already occurred and continues. This work is evident in many parts of the country and world and needs to be claimed, celebrated, and more widely implemented.

Three Options

With regards to stigma, it seems to me that people with a mental retardation label and their allies have three general options to consider. The first option is to accept the status-quo and do nothing different. Unfortunately, choosing this option will involve acquiescing to existing social arrangements and ignoring the debilitating impact that stigma has on people's lives. Can we, in good conscience, accept this option? I am convinced that we cannot! At the very least, we must help the people who are labeled consider their alternatives?

A second option is to expand our efforts in helping some people disengage from the mental retardation world. The goal would be to help them become less stigmatized and more accepted in society. This option may involve "passing" or shedding the mental retardation label. Unfortunately, passing is only available to people who have relatively unobtrusive disability attributes and a capacity to conceal this aspect of their identity. Nevertheless, the option of passing must be made available to those who can become the beneficiaries. The moral aspects of passing must also be considered, but labeled people should be helped to determine what they believe is right for them to do.

A third option is to fight for the elimination of stigma. The self-advocacy movement, countless exceptional agencies, and many individual advocates are leading the way in pursuing this option. Unfortunately, the mental retardation system has not yet discovered the central role that it can play in this fight.

Fighting for social change can bring a whole new order to relations among people with and without disabilities. Labels can become less important to our work, and the stigma associated with disabilities can be greatly diminished. Most important, people with a mental retardation label can be more accepted as equals in all of our lives. Negative distinctions can fade away and our diversity can become increasingly appreciated and celebrated.

Eventually, this third option will lead to a time when people with disabilities can freely identify this aspect of who they are without being stereotyped, demeaned, or ignored. In short, eliminating stigma can bring many profound positive changes to our social world.

In the long run, if people become successfully integrated into society through advocacy, passing will no longer be a relevant option. However, my sense is that the stigma problems associated with cognitive disabilities in our society have existed for too long to go away easily. Thus, the option of passing may be the only realistic way for some people to achieve societal inclusion in the immediate years ahead.

Options two and three do not have to be mutually exclusive strategies for allies who want to help labeled people. However, labeled people will ultimately have to choose one strategy or the other. A major conflict seems inevitable between being a visible, outspoken leader of the self-advocacy movement and attempting to disappear into the mainstream. Furthermore, each of these strategies demands more than enough time and energy to preclude attempts by labeled people to take on both strategies at the same time.

Stigma and Other Groups of People

Another closing thought seems important to mention. Stigma is a problem faced by many groups, not just people with a mental retardation label. Goffman (1963) reminds us of three general categories of stigmatized people—racial, ethnic, and religious minorities; people behaving in ways that are contrary to societal norms; and people with "physical blemishes."

Many other people have stigma problems that are similar to those encountered by people with a mental retardation label. Examples include people with physical disabilities, mental illness, and AIDS; people who are obese; and gays and lesbians. Some of the ways that stigma can be confronted and overcome are similar as well. For example, members of all of these groups may need to do "private work" to gain awareness and understanding of their "differentness" and its connections to stigma. Confronting stigma through a self-advocacy movement is a pertinent agenda for all of these groups. Developing and maintaining friendships with people outside of one's group are central to survival and fulfillment. Also, passing is an option for many in each of these groups to consider.

Unfortunately, all of these groups have a tendency to stratify their members based on the degree of each person's differentness. For example, among people with physical disabilities, those with hearing impairments perceive themselves as less stigmatized than those with visual impairments, and those with visual impairments feel superior to those who use a wheelchair.

Because the problem of stigma effects a much larger number than those who are the focus of this book, why not encourage all of these stigmatized groups to join together to combat stigma? Unfortunately, there are many formidable barriers preventing such a potentially powerful alliance. One barrier is a long history of working in isolation of each other. Another barrier is the advantage of going it alone and seeking redress just for one's own group. A need to promote stratification is another principal reason why these groups do not work together. Stigmatized groups stratify themselves in relation to other stigmatized groups, and people with mental retardation labels are among the least desired.

Looking ahead, new visions are needed if we are to have a significant influence on the future. Imagine an enormously powerful movement of people with many different stigmatizing conditions joining together to claim all of their rights. Maybe, this is the time to plant the seed for such a movement.

References

Graney, B. (1996). Thoughts on the death of a valiant self-advocate. In Dybwad, G., & Bersani, H. (Ed.). *New Voices: Self-advocacy by people with disabilities.* Cambridge, MA: Brookline Books.

Goffman, E. (1963). *Stigma: Notes on the management of spoiled identity.* Englewood Cliffs, NJ: Prentice-Hall.

NAME INDEX

SUBJECT INDEX